My Ministry Is Where
My Misery Was

My Ministry Is Where My Misery Was

My Ministry Is Where My Misery Was

Mrs. Agatha Amoateng-Boahen

My Ministry Is Where My Misery Was

Dr. Gabriel Amoateng-Boahen

My Ministry Is Where My Misery Was

My Ministry Is Where My Misery Was
All Rights Reserved

Copyright © 2016 by Gabriel Amoateng-Boahen

No part of this publication may be reproduced, stored in a retrieval system or transmitted in any way by any means, electronic, mechanical, photocopy, digital imaging, recording or otherwise, without the prior written permission of the author who is the copyright owner, except as provided by USA copyright law.

Bible references are taken from the various translations of the Bible as stated.

Author's Contact: *gabriel.ab925@yahoo.com*
gabrielabm1913@gmail.com

The opinions expressed by the author in this book are not necessarily the opinion and views of Rehoboth House.

Paperback: 978-1-68411-312-5
Hardcover: 978-1-68411-313-2

Published in the United States of America by
Rehoboth House, Chicago.
rehobothhouseonline.com

REHOBOTH HOUSE

My Ministry Is Where My Misery Was

Table of contents

Synopsis Of My Books..*i*

Dedication..*xi*

Acknowledgment..*xiii*

Preface..*xv*

Abstract..*xix*

Chapter 1: Reflecting on The Source Of Ministry And Passion..................1

The Genesis of the Topic..1

What Is Ministry.?..2

The Interconnectedness Between One's Past and Present Ministry..................2

The "Culture of Silence" Promoted Domestic Violence Growing Up..................4

The Unheard Voice Suffers in Silence and Pain..5

The Time to Speak Up for Others..5

Meaningful Education Should Benefit the Underprivileged..7

Chapter 2: Some Personalities Who Went From Misery To Ministry..................9

Tim Ryan..10

Rodney Perez..12

Horatio Gates Spafford..14

John Newton..17

Reflection on the Genesis of Your Ministry..20

Chapter 3: The Hidden Pain Gave Birth To The Ministry..................21

The Present Ministry is Traceable to Past Pain..21

My Passion for Ministry is Advocacy and Bridge Building..................................22

The Silent Majority Must Also Be Heard..23

Many Are Dying in Their Homes..24

This is The Time to "Unveil" the Curtain for Transparency...25

Chapter 4: The "Culture Of Silence" Must End...27

The Culture Itself Imprisons the Individual...27

The Church Must Take the Lead..28

Leadership to Embrace Critical Feedback..29

It Is About Issues Not Personalities..30

Constructive Criticism Promotes Growth and Development....................................31

A Lesson for Individuals, Families, Churches, Communities, and Nations..............32

Chapter 5: The Misery Cannot Persist..33

The Minister Speaks to End the Misery in the Heart of Many..................................33

Many Die Silently Out of Misery on Daily Basis...36

Society Will Not Forgive Those Who Compromise..37

The Concerned Leader Thinks About the Next Generation.....................................38

The Minister is God's Mouthpiece...43

Chapter 6: A New Dawn Of Hope...47

A New Dawn of Hope Is Here Now..47

Injustices and Myriads of Abuses Among Humanity Must Cease.............................48

The Loving Father Cares..50

All Join Hands to Fight "Culture of Silence," Domestic violence, and Injustices/Abuses..51

Identify and Address the Misery in Your Ministry Intentionally...............................53

The "Heavenly Call" Demands Accountability to Oneself, Other, and God............53

Conclusion: Spirituality, Ministry, Misery, Compassion, And Passion....................55

Deep Faith and Spirituality Confront Human Injustices...55

The Spirit of Courage and Boldness 56

Contemporary Ministry Must Address Diverse Misery and Pain/Abuses.....................57

Compassion for People...57

Passion for Ministry..58

Prayers Of Salvation..61

Rededication...63

Author's Profile...65

Recommended Books..77

How To Order Copies Of My Books/Donations..80

My Ministry Is Where My Misery Was

Synopsis of My 10 BOOKS

Book 1: *Integral Pastoral Care In Ghana: Proposals For Healing In The Asante Context*

What is "Pastoral Care"? Many authorities differently define Pastoral Care. The Encyclopedia of Christianity defines it as the ministry of care and counseling by pastors, chaplains, and other religious leaders to members of their church or congregation, or to anyone within institutional settings, with a focus on healing, reconciling, guiding, and sustaining.

Kate Stone Lombardi, in her article, titled "Chaplains as Comforters," in the New York Times of July 20, 2003, says, "While doctors and nurses at the Westchester Medical Center here work on the bodies of patients, there is another group of people – the hospital chaplains, who work with their spirits." She lists some of the many services provided by the Pastoral Care Giver in a hospital setting as enumerated in my book and concludes on the note that "Chaplains see human emotions at their raw... They work with people whose bodies are ravaged... These Chaplains say that to see a medical crisis brings on a spiritual crisis.

Book 2: *The "Culture Of Silence" Contributes To Perpetuating Domestic Violence: A Case Study Of Family Life In The Brong Ahafo Region Of Ghana*

The main topic for the research is domestic violence with women and children as the apparent victims; the perpetrators and the bystanders in the community are the key players. The interviewees are Catholic couples from the Brong Ahafo Region of Ghana and now living in Chicago. Their experiences (Chapter 1) based on scientific analysis with statistical figures enriched the research. The Ghanaian culture (Chapter 2) is good but at the same time has certain aspects that are abusive to many in their families. The "culture of silence" is thus entrenched in the very culture.

Komonchak, Cozzens, the African Synod, the Ghana Bishops' Conference and other writers on the Catholic Church (Chapter 3) raised interesting but crucial issues for consideration to bring about healthy church life and overall positive change in Ghana as a whole and the Brong Ahafo Region in particular. The Pastoral Response (Chapter 5) has available local resources for the victim, the perpetrator, the family, the church, the community/bystanders, and the nation/Ghana. The outcome of the above engagement with my audience calls for a new praxis that is positive and transformative for societal growth.

Book 3: *Spiritual Mentorship For Pastors And Church Leaders Today*

My timely book seeks to, among others, appreciate and congratulate all men and women of God in ministry, and encourage them for their continued dedication in leading the flock under their care as "Chief Shepherds." Bravo! On a more concerned and passionate note, the book seeks to equip the pastor/leader with some basic ministerial skills for sound, fruitful, untiring, and ever-lasting soul-impacting ministry, devoid of any abuses either covertly or overtly. My other aim is to challenge the pastor/leader to be professional and current for contemporary ministry because society is becoming more scientific, technological, academic, intellectual, argumentative, and above all, critical and skeptical. Our local communities are increasingly becoming more violent, confused, frustrated, socially darker and gloomy, stressful, and uncontrollable. The pastoral services of the pastoral leaders thus become inevitable, crucial, and critical because communities look up to the spiritual leader.

Book 4: *Testimonies Today Tributes Tomorrow*

When all three phenomena, namely, culture, theology, and spirituality, work harmoniously in the life of the believer, balance – physical, emotional, and spiritual stability is the outcome. Peace and joy within oneself, self-confidence, respect, and love for God and humans lead to satisfaction, as well as hopeful and faithful (faith in God) life, all of which will eventually result in a compelling soul-impacting life and great testimony. This kind of testimony is easily seen, read, and either written by others (biography) or self-written (autobiography). The individual must hear the testimony today, but not as a tribute at death tomorrow. So, I say, "Testimonies Today Tributes Tomorrow."

Book 5: Pastoral Care & Holistic Ministry: The Dynamics Of The Private Life, The Professional Life & The Public Life Of The Pastor/Leader

To be pastoral is to create a sacred space and time for the other person who needs support. The caregiver is fully present, listening critically and attentively to locate the "pastoral pillars" on the way for continued support. The pastoral caregiver should identify the root causes and pertinent, disturbing issues emanating from the body, soul, and spirit of the receiver of pastoral care. The book also focuses on the private, professional, and public lives of pastoral caregivers- pastors, church leaders, chaplains, counselors, psychotherapists, clinical social workers, spiritual directors, health professionals, and similarly- situated others.

> May God Himself, the God of peace, sanctify you through and through. May your whole spirit, soul, and body be kept blameless until our Lord Jesus Christ comes again (1 Thess. 5:23, NIV).

Book 6: My Ministry Is Where My Misery Was

Two words clearly stand out in the book title – "Ministry" and "Misery." Two of my earlier books, "Spiritual Mentorship For Pastors and Church Leaders Today" and Pastoral Care and Holistic Ministry: The Private, Professional, and Public Lives of the Pastor/Leader," have intensely dealt with and expatiated on ministry as a subject. I also discussed how the individual minister should respond to God's Call upon one's life, and the many challenges associated with the Call.

This book simply narrows the discussion to ministers who went through personal problems and challenges of life, which eventually gave birth to their present ministries. There are many such ministries out there, probably including yours. I am personally touched by the ministry of Tim Ryan, to whom I have dedicated this book to honor and appreciate for availing himself to be used of the Lord in setting free from all forms of addiction, many people, especially the youth in our homes, communities, schools, churches, and in many countries. Tim powerfully shares his personal testimony of liberation from addiction with many today. Thus, his present ministry was his past misery.

> "But as for you, you meant evil against me; but God meant it for good, in order to bring it about as it is this day, to serve many people alive"(Gen. 50:20, NKJV). Joseph's past misery became his ministry that liberated an entire nation to the glory of God.

Book 7: *The Controlling Power Of The Mind: Renewing Your Mind Unto Victory*

According to James N. Watkins, "A river is able to cut through a rock not because it is powerful, but because of its persistency." Persistent use of the brain is a great asset for both human and societal development. The book unearths what the best brain can do, especially when it is subjected to the authority of God's Word, and is inspired and led by the Holy Spirit. As you read the book, you will find hidden revelation of the controlling power of the mind. In view of this, the author asks the question: What is the wealthiest place in the world in relation to the mind?

The author lifts high the "banner" of the best brain, saying, "Abundant natural resources do not necessarily develop a nation; best brains do. The controlling power of the mind is unimaginable and impacts our everyday lives. The time to renew your mind unto victory is NOW.

Book 8: *African Punctuality": Time Is Divine And Of The Greatest Essence*

The title of this book has evolved through my critical observation over the years about how some Africans, both home and in the diaspora, handle time. Time is central, critical, and crucial to our human existence. The Creator- God respected time very much in the creation account in Genesis Chapters 1 and 2. Time maximization and utilization leads to development and progress. Conversely, the misuse and misappropriation of time are "friendly" to poverty. The twenty-four hours divided into three segments of discussion and analysis in this book of mine tell the full story. What is "African Punctuality?" It is more than you think. Read more about it in this book.

Lord Chesterfield, a British Statesman (1694-1773), says, "Know the true value of time, snatch, seize, and enjoy every moment of it. No idleness, no laziness, no procrastination. Never put off till tomorrow what you can do today. Whatever is worth doing at all is worth doing well. I recommend you to take care of the minutes, for the hours will take care of themselves."

Book 1: The Theology Of My Life: From Kintampo To Chicago

The rationale behind the book title is simply to prove the faithfulness of God in my life as I chronologically chronicle and trace how far He has brought me. I am forever greatly grateful and thankful to God for how he has ordered every step of mine right from my mother's womb in seclusion. Like the Prophet Jeremiah, God foreknew me before I was born (Jer. 1:50).

Among other things, the book establishes the fact that the plan of God (Jer. 29:11) will always prevail and manifest to God's glory and honor regardless of any human encumbrances and challenges. Precisely, it charts my life's journey from Kintampo in the Brong Ahafo Region of Ghana to Chicago, Illinois, USA, indicating the major "theological pillars" on the way. It also locates and emphasizes the God story/factor (theology) from one accomplishment to another, not discounting the challenges that accompanied each success story.

Oswald Chambers, a twentieth century Scottish Baptist and Holiness-Movement evangelist and teacher, best known for the devotional, My Utmost for His Highest, tells us that Faith never knows where it is being led, but it loves and knows the One who is leading. Where will you spend eternity: heaven or hell? The author asks the reader respectfully. The book ends with a quote from Abraham Lincoln: "My concern is not whether God is on our side: My greatest concern is to be on God's side, for God is always right."

Book 10: The Theology Of Telephone Technology Today

The art of sending messages and communicating with each other is as old as the human race. It all started with our first parents, Adam and Eve (Gen. 3), and has evolved over time. Different generations had their way of sending messages, which worked perfectly at the time. For example, in traditional Africa in general and Ghana in particular, chiefs in the past sent important messages through their linguists ("Akyeame," as they are called in Akan, a major Ghanaian unwritten language). From letter writing, we moved to the telegram technology.

I believe that the old folks reading this book remember the "good old days" of sending a telegram (Morse code), with its accompanying fears and anxieties at the receiving end. From the telegram era came the fax machine generation, which was welcomed with amazement and astonishment at the time. Then came the "electronic-mail era," which has profoundly and positively impacted humanity with information technology to promote local, national, and international businesses and transactions. For sure, we are on a continued journey with the Creator God, who directs us to new inventions, discoveries, researches, technologies, and developments.

Over time, sending messages has undergone dramatic and speedy metamorphosis to the amazement of all in the 21st century. Undoubtedly, technologically, our generation is the most blessed. I will in no way overlook or undervalue the God factor in all of this, hence the word "theology" in my book title to emphasize the centrality of "Divine Presence" in the acquisition of knowledge by humanity, especially during the end times as prophesied by Daniel (Dan. 12:4).

Throughout the book, the author establishes the fact that God continuously searches for humanity for reconciliation, and the process demands a daily response and fellowship with Him through Bible study, prayer, and a life of holiness. It highlights the multiplicity of social, economic, and spiritual advantages and disadvantages of telephone technology, which networks with other systems to enhance efficiency and progress diversely.

Indeed, the author speaks to the heart cry of God as he dials his "telephone of repentance" and pleads passionately with humans to respond to His love and the salvation provided in John 3:16

> **"For God so loved the world, that he gave his only begotten Son, that whoever believeth in Him should not perish, but have everlasting life (KIV).**

The telephone number to Heaven is found in the book of Jeremiah 33:3:

> **"Call to me and I will answer you and tell you great and unsearchable things you do not know."**

My Ministry Is Where My Misery Was

Dedication

I dedicate this book to Tim Ryan whose ministry was born out of the misery he went through with every form and shape of addiction for years. Today, Tim shares his personal deliverance story with statistics and empirical evidence, that portrays the damaging effect of addiction to our communities through his ministry, "A Man in Recovery Foundation." About the book title, I could not have dedicated it to any person other than Tim Ryan; my brother in the Lord.

My Ministry Is Where My Misery Was

Acknowledgment

My image of ministry is the "Midwife." The midwife companions the pregnant woman until the baby is born safely. On my journey of ministry, I became "the pregnant woman" who needed the urgent assistance of the "midwife." In the days of misery, pain, sleepless nights, persecution of a sort in ministry, and challenging academic pursuits, the Lord used many "midwives" to support me in the "labor room" physically, emotionally, and spiritually. To all such "midwives," too many to name, I pause, to reflect on your support, and express my deepest gratitude and profound appreciation for your prayer support and encouragement in my ministry.

Few of such "midwives"/friends are: Mr. and Mrs. SB Nsankyire, Mr. and Mrs. Joseph Antwi Agyei, Mr. and Mrs. Dave Annor Sakyi, Rev. and Mrs. Moses K. Kyeremeh, Rev. and Mrs. Kwadwo Owusu Sarpong, Mr. and Mrs. George Boakye, Dr. and Mrs. Charles Kwadwo Boadi Kessey, Prof. and Mrs. KD Kessey, Rev. and Mrs. Joe Gyansa-Lutterodt, Mr. and Mrs. Samuel Nsowah, Mr. and Mrs. Robert Nsiah, Mr. and Rev.

(Mrs.) Isaac Nsowah Arhin, Rev. Dr. and Mrs. Jacob Atuahene Nsowaah, Mr. and Mrs. Dave Anane Druyeh, Mr. and Mrs. Sampson Amofa Kra, Evang. and Mrs. Nuamah Kankam, Mr. and Mrs. Richard Osei, Mr. and Mrs. Emmanuel Opoku Awuah, Mr. and Mrs. James Oppong Owusu, Mr. and Mrs. JWK Edusei, Mr. and Mrs. George Kumi, Mr. and Mrs. Anthony Osei Assibey, Mr. and Mrs. Emmanuel Mawuli Tamakloe, Bishop and Mrs. Osei Bonsu Nsiah, Mr. and Mrs. Solomon Amoateng, Mr. and Mrs. Augustine Afriyie, Mr. and Mrs. Anthony Sarfo Kwateng, Dr. and Mrs. George Assibey-Mensah, Rev. Dr. and Mrs. Kofi Noonoo, Mn. and Mrs. Nicholas Thompson, Rev. and Mrs. Dzifanu Agbenya, Dr. and Mrs. Maxwell Nartey, Rev. and Mrs. Samuel Obeng, Dr. and Mrs. James Erbowor-Becksen, Rev. Dr. and Dr.(Mrs.) Ramble Ankumah, Rev.Dr. Mary Adufah, Dr. and Mrs. Samuel Gorman Awuah, Dr. and Mrs. Mark Nimo, Mr. and Mrs. Donatus Kotogbor, Mr. and Mrs. Charles Owusu Ansah, Ms. Josephine Serwaa, Nana and Mrs. Yaw Adu Gyamfi, Mr. and Nana Abena Pokuaa, Mr. Brian Murphy, and Mr. David Schmid.

May the God of peace, love, comfort, and amazing performance, expand your territories and bless your family, profession, ministry, aspirations, hopes, and deep-seated intentions.

My deep appreciation as always goes to my wife, Mrs. Agatha Amoateng-Boahen, and our dear children and their respective families for your diverse support.

I extend my final gratitude to my publisher, Rev. Emeka Joshua Emeruem, Rehoboth House, Chicago, Illinois, USA.

Preface

Two words clearly stand out in the title of this book: "Ministry and Misery." Ministry is serving God's people everywhere by the pastoral caregiver. Two of my earlier books, "Spiritual Mentorship For Pastors and Church Leaders Today" and Pastoral Care and Holistic Ministry, have extensively dealt with and expatiated on ministry as a subject. I also discussed how a minister responds to God's call upon his or her life and the challenges associated with the call.

This book simply narrows the discussion to ministers who went through personal problems and difficulties of life and out of which gave birth to their present ministries. There are many of such ministers out there, probably including yours. The ministry of Tim Ryan has touched me personally. Therefore, I have dedicated this book to him, to honor and appreciate him for availing himself to be used of the Lord to set many free from various forms of addictions especially the youth, in our homes, churches, schools, communities, and countries around the globe. Tim powerfully shares his personal testimony of liberation from addiction with many today. Thus, his present ministry was his past misery.

Tim tells his personal addictions for about fourteen years until his liberation by the Lord Jesus Christ through the inspiration and power of the Holy Spirit. Tim's ministry is "A Man in Recovery Foundation" based in Naperville, Illinois, USA, was his past misery. Tim's motto is: "From Dope to Hope." I listened to him at the Trinity Broadcasting Network (TBN) on Saturday, May 21, 2106, and I was inspired to engage some of his research findings in this book for my readers to draw inspiration from. Examples: parents who are seeking liberation for their children, children worried and concerned about their parents' addiction, a spouse in search of freedom for the other partner, a pastor desperately praying to help church members, and yet still, professors who interact with students who suffer from addictions on the university campuses. To extend the same urgent message of liberation to our streets cannot be overemphasized because many of the street violence is traceable to drug, substance or alcoholic abuse and addiction. I will also consult other advocates and liberation "activists" like Rodney Perez and the "Joy in Our Town" program by TBN.

Addiction is no respecter of persons. Like the "culture of silence" and domestic violence, it can affect and infect every member of our family, church, school, social club, community, or country. Both the addicted and the free member of society need help from addiction and its dire consequences and resources for the liberated to companion the addicted. Nothing is more frustrating than wanting to help but unable due to the complexities of the problem and a lack of possible human and materials resources and logistics.

Preface

Another outstanding ministry whose operations tie into the book title is "Operation Promise, which is a reality of the consequences of texting and driving, drinking and driving, and drug addiction. Operation Promise was established in 2009 and incorporated in 2013. The volunteer team is comprised of students, school administrators and parents from seven community and private High Schools, along with multiple municipalities, emergency responders, and county judicial system throughout central and northern Illinois. Team Promise's goal is opening eyes and saving lives through awareness and education by professional filmmaking of the reality of the pressures and addictions that children and adults face in today's society.

A film production of Operation Promise 2016 was viewed during a free community event at LP Township High School, LaSalle, Illinois, on April 20th, 2016 at 7:00 pm. Afterward, it was shared with schools throughout the United States upon request. Rodney Perez is the President and Founder of Operation Promise.

The great work by Operation Promise stands to serve a dual purpose: Awareness creation through performance, and liberating many, especially, the youth and young adults. I am not discounting the benefits the adults, parents, and professionals who teach and train these young ones can derive from this initiative.

Adding a spiritual component to any liberation program for addiction will hasten the liberation process for the addicted individual. Some of the liberated victims of addiction are likely to turn around to establish ministries and foundations to help others as well. Addiction is an umbrella word that encapsulates various addictive behaviors like food, sleep, sex, work without rest (workaholic), alcohol, drugs, and related substances and forms of addiction (anger, inferiority or superiority complex, phobias, the list continues).

The author now invites the reader to reflect on the motivating factors that gave birth to one's ministry. Probably, your ministry is where your ministry was.

Abstract

Two words clearly stand out in the title of this book: "Ministry and Misery." Ministry is serving God's people everywhere by the pastoral caregiver. Two of my earlier books, "Spiritual Mentorship For Pastors and Church Leaders Today" and Pastoral Care and Holistic Ministry, have extensively dealt with and expatiated on ministry as a subject. I also discussed how a minister responds to God's call upon his or her life and the challenges associated with the call.

This book streamlines the discussion to ministers who went through personal challenges in life and out of which gave birth to their present ministries. There are many of such ministers out there, probably including you. The ministry of Tim Ryan has touched me personally. Therefore, I have dedicated this book to him, to honor and appreciate him for availing himself to be used of the Lord to set many free from various forms of addictions especially the youth, in our homes, churches, schools, communities, and countries around the globe. Tim powerfully shares his personal testimony of liberation from addiction with many today. Thus, his present ministry was his past misery.

My Ministry Is Where My Misery Was

CHAPTER 1

Reflecting On The Source Of Ministry And Passion

The Genesis of the Topic

There is a direct correlation between one's ministry and past life. For example, the individual lost one's mother at birth, and therefore, grows up as an orphan without maternal love and care, and so, establishes an orphanage to cater for school children without parents.

Olaudah Equiano (c.1745-1796) was eleven years old when he was kidnapped and sold into slavery. He made the harrowing journey from West Africa to the West Indies, then to the colony of Virginia, and finally to England. He eventually purchased his freedom when he was twenty years old, still bearing the emotional and physical scars of the inhumane treatment he had experienced. Equiano was unable to enjoy his freedom while others were still enslaved. Therefore, he became active in the movement to abolish slavery in England. Thus, his misery later became his ministry (Source: Our Daily Bread, August 31, 2016). His experience agrees with the divine mandate God gave to the Jews on their way to the Promised Land.

> "Remember the command that Moses the servant of the Lord gave you: 'The Lord your God is giving you rest and has granted you this land.' ...You are to help your brothers until the Lord gives them rest, as he has done for you, and until they too have taken possession of the land that the Lord your God is giving them. After that, you may go back and occupy your own land, which Moses the servant of the Lord gave you east of the Jordan toward the sunrise" (Josh. 1:13-15, NIV).

John Newton with a bitter childhood experience on the sea, as a former slave master, and later a clergyman, advocated for the abolition of slave trade in England.

Many today are in ministry because of their painful past. Some can consciously establish the link between their ministry and their past pain and misery, while others may not. Better still, others are aware, but they do not want to revisit their painful past.

This book aims at helping every minister to boldly speak about their past with the intent to positively impact lives through their respective ministries and testimonies. Robert Morris, Founding Senior Pastor of Gateway Church, a multi-campus church in the Dallas, Fort Worth, Metroplex, without shame, boldly speaks openly about his past immoral life and addiction to encourage his congregation and audience. His book "From Dream to Destiny" has his full story. Get a copy and read it.

His ministry that began in the year 2000 had grown to more than 36, 000 active members. Robert Morris features on the weekly television program, The Blessed Life. At present, he serves as chairman of the board of The King's University. He is a bestselling author of fourteen books including The Blessed Life, The God I Never Knew, Truly Free, and Frequency; and also a renowned American television preacher at the Trinity Broadcasting Network (TBN).

What is Ministry?

Ministry is service to God, His people and humanity in general, everywhere and at any given time by the servant-leader or minister of God. This service takes many forms. It could be a ministry to patients, veterans, prisoners, children, youth and young adults, men, women, orphans, alcoholics, pastors and church leaders. The list continues. The minister has a divine mandate to shepherd and account for the souls of individuals and groups under his leadership. Like any profession, the minister needs competent and basic training to function efficiently (Read my book" Spiritual Mentorship for Pastors and Church Leaders Today").

> "Have confidence in your leaders and submit to their authority, because they keep watch over you as those who must give an account. Do this so that their work will be a joy, not a burden, for that would be of no benefit to you" (Heb. 13:17, NIV).

The Interconnectedness Between One's Past and Present Ministry

Some ministers are very much alert and conscious of the genesis of their calling and the correlation between their painful past and present ministry. These ministers preach with simplicity, clarity, confidence, and boldness because their life journey attests to their ministry. They minister from their painful past, the pivotal point of their liberation, and the turnaround they experienced in the process. Differently put, they minister from liberation theology that cannot be silent about his or her liberation. Thus, we are liberated to liberate others, saved to save others, and rescued to rescue others. Others, on the other hand, minister "historically" as they tell their life story about God's calling upon their lives. In both instances, the past painful experiences positively affect their present ministry as the point of conversion is highlighted for the person to be ministered to.

The "Culture of Silence" Promoted Domestic Violence and Abuses Growing Up

The "culture of silence" is ingrained in many cultures. Africa/Ghana is a classic example. I can still not make head or tail of why certain abuses go on in our compound family house and the neighborhood without bringing the perpetrators to justice. African/Ghanaian culture, though has many positive traits and features, inadvertently promotes the "culture of silence," which further perpetuates domestic violence and other abuses. I suffered bullying and beating by some adult members of our family, but no one addressed the said abuse to bring the culprits to book. However, for the timely intervention of some bystanders, some of us would have suffered permanent deformity. Many equally suffered abuses of various degrees in their marriage and family lives. The African culture which is patriarchal and male-dominated empowered the men to abuse their wives for no apparent and justifiable reason. This childhood observation and concern gave birth to my second book titled The "Culture of Silence" Contributes to Perpetuating Domestic Violence: A Case Study of Family Life in the Brong Ahafo Region of Ghana. Thus, my Ministry is Where My Misery Was.

The Unheard Voice Suffers in Silence and Pain

Sadly, the hushed unheard voice dies silently in our midst. The unspeakable truth is to speak out now and protect the vulnerable and powerless from every form and shape of abuse. We must be honest and confront the brutal facts. Many are hurting in our society that is unseen or unheard. We must address this disparity and injustice on a broad spectrum.

We must engage in meaningful socio-economic programs that at the end of the day, must benefit the society, especially, the downtrodden who are at the lowest level at the "societal ladder." Lemuel advises all of us.

> "Speak up for those who cannot speak for themselves; ensure justice for those being crushed" (Prov. 31:8, NLT).

This book among others aims at establishing a simple and truthful fact- there are many unheard voices, who suffer silently and in pain among us. At any point along the way, are many of such people in our homes, families, neighborhoods, communities, villages, towns, cities, schools, churches, ministries, institutions, workplaces, and countries. The time to speak up is now!

The Time to Speak Up for Others is Now

My book invites you to look around and identify any social construct that is affecting and infecting the voiceless in your local community. In your small way, pray for the grace and practical wisdom to confront the issues with the intent of effecting a positive change to benefit the defenseless majority. The silent majority always suffer in any given human community or institution. For example, in some countries, only the ten percent wealthy few control ninety percent of human and natural resources, whereas the ninety percent majority poor share the meager ten percent of the available human and natural resources. This cycle has existed and continued for years. The society has unfortunately accepted it as the norm in everyday life.

The time to wake up and speak about any identifiable political, social, economic, and religious injustices is now. It is sad to remark that when it comes to taxation, the ten percent wealthy few that controls ninety percent of the nation's wealth in some countries, especially in developing countries, evade paying taxes proportionately. Sadly, the defenseless ninety percent poor that control the meager ten percent of the nation's resources pay taxes from the exact proportion of their income. Therefore, it is no wonder that some countries are poor.

No one is "untouchable" except God, and therefore, pray for the courage to speak out boldly. "Unspeakable Truth" as empowered by Priscilla Hayner in her book: Unspeakable Truths: Confronting State Terror and Atrocity. Nelson Mandela of South Africa in another development believed that one of the most powerful means to bring about change is through education. From a humble beginning, he went to London to study law, returned to his country to establish the first law firm by a black South African to effect change. In the process, he had to spend twenty-seven years of his life in prison. In the end, his misery (Pain in Prison) became his "Ministry" (Political Emancipation of Black South Africans) and eventually liberated his country from the cruel and obnoxious apartheid regime.

Meaningful Education Should Benefit the Underprivileged

Modern scientific education should identify, address, and solve the myriad of human problems that confront us daily. In other words, education must be human-related in all ramification. More funding should be channeled into scientific research that will empower the weak and defenseless in the society, and uplift their living standard. Education should not be the privilege for the rich few but must be affordable by all regardless of one's social status and background. More professional teachers should be trained to informally teach others ("Night School"/ Literacy Classes in Ghana in those days) and through the formal educational system (From Nursery, Kindergarten, Primary, Elementary, High School, College, and Universities). Sound education has a direct correlation on healthy living- good diet, exercising, avoiding preventable diseases by observing simple basic hygiene, and others.

Those of us with access to formal and advanced knowledge should help our less fortunate brothers and sisters in society while waiting for all to receive the basic and formal education. Again, the educational system must be relevant to human development through job acquisition to support oneself and family, and to contribute to the Gross National Product (GDP). Producing half-baked and unemployable graduates adds "fuel to the burning fire of poverty" in most countries.

As the book title suggests and my simple definition of ministry states, it is service to advocating for excellent education. This service becomes "ministry" for those who have experienced poverty, but by divine help, ascend to the top academically and professionally. The book is more about identifying one's past pain and how God intervened in their lives and wrought deliverance, thereby turning their misery into ministry to help those who are struggling for liberation. Together we strive to succeed (TD Jakes at TBN), and Hand in Hand Transforming Lives Positively (Royal Diadem Pastoral Center Motto).

CHAPTER 2

Some Personalities Who Went From Misery To Ministry

There are many figures I can discuss in this section of the book, but for the sake of time and space, I have chosen to discuss few of them. These people at a point in time in their lives went through a period of life challenges but timely divine intervention "rescued" them. These people have become reference points and a source of hope and encouragement for those going through similar problems they experienced. Some of them were addicted to habits but later realized the physical, emotional, and spiritual consequences of their behaviors. In the deepest of their hearts, they possibly said something like what the Apostle Paul stated in the book of Romans when he had internal struggles with his flesh and couldn't comprehend why:

> "I do not understand myself at all, for I really want to do what is right, but I can't. I do what I don't want to-what I hate (Rom. 7:15)."

Most people who suffer from addiction, down deep in their hearts, resonate with the heart cry of Paul.

I present for the reader's reflection some of these individuals who had their moments of trial and misery, which eventually turned out to be their ministries. Today, they are a great source of hope and encouragement to many who read about them. In the ensuing paragraphs are few of such personalities.

Tim Ryan

I listened to Tim Ryan at the Trinity Broadcasting Network (TBN) and read more about him. His openness and present ministry deeply touched me. Tim tells about his personal addictions for about 14 years until his liberation by the powerful presence of the Lord Jesus Christ, our savior and redeemer, through the inspiration and conviction of the Holy Spirit. Tim's ministry is "A Man in Recovery Foundation" based in Naperville, Illinois, USA. Tim's motto reads "From Dope to Hope."

As I listened to Tim at TBN on Saturday, May 21, 2016, I had the strongest conviction to engage some of his research findings in this book as I mentioned previously in the Preface. The quote from the Apostle Paul in Romans 7:15 above supports the claim that behind every form of addiction is the element of spirituality -spiritual bondage that enslaves the individual. Addiction should not only be limited to substance abuse. There are as many forms of addictions as there are many people who suffer from them.

Here are some common forms of addiction below:

1. Drug Addiction
2. Alcohol Addiction
3. Gambling Addiction
4. Sex Addiction
5. Internet Addiction
6. Shopping Addiction
7. Video Game Addiction
8. Plastic Surgery Addiction
9. Binge Eating Disorders: Food Addiction
10. Sleep Addiction
11. Work Addiction
12. Exercising Addiction
13. Pornography (attaining, viewing)
14. Television Addiction (a particular "bad" program)
15. Spiritual obsession (as opposed to religious devotion)
16. Pain (pain- seeking becomes an addictive behavior)
17. Cutting ("Self-harm can become addictive. It may start off as an impulse or something you do to feel more in control, but soon it feels like the cutting or self –harming is controlling you. It often turns into a compulsive behavior that seems impossible to control and stop.")

Source: www.helpguide.org.>articles>anxiety

Rodney Pezez

To extend the same urgent message of liberation to our streets cannot be overemphasized because many of the street violence is traceable to drug, substance or alcoholic abuse and addiction. I will also consult other advocates and liberation "activists" like Rodney Pezez and the "Joy in Our Town" program.

Addiction is no respecter of persons. Like the "culture of silence" and domestic violence, it can affect and infect every member of our family, church, school, social club, community, or country. Both the addicted and the free member of society need help from addiction and its dire consequences and resources for the liberated to companion the addicted. Nothing is more frustrating than wanting to help but unable due to the complexities of the problem and a lack of possible human and materials resources and logistics.

Another outstanding ministry whose operations tie into the book title is "Operation Promise," which is a reality of the consequences of texting and driving, drinking and driving, and drug addiction. Operation Promise was established in 2009 and incorporated in 2013. The volunteer team is comprised of students, school administrators and parents from seven community and private High Schools, along with multiple municipalities, emergency responders, and county judicial system throughout central and northern Illinois. Team Promise's goal is opening eyes and saving lives through awareness and education by professional filmmaking of the reality of the pressures and addictions that children and adults face in today's society.

A film production of Operation Promise 2016 was viewed during a free community event at LP Township High School,

LaSalle, Illinois, on April 20th, 2016 at 7:00 pm. Afterward, it was shared with schools throughout the United States upon request. Rodney Pezez is the President and Founder of Operation Promise.

The great work by Operation Promise stands to serve a dual purpose: Awareness creation through performance, and liberating many, especially, the youth and young adults. I am not discounting the benefits the adults, parents, and professionals who teach and train these young ones can derive from this initiative.

Adding a spiritual component to any liberation program for addiction will hasten the liberation process for the addicted individual. Some of the liberated victims of addiction are likely to turn around to establish ministries and foundations to help others as well. Addiction is an umbrella word that encapsulates various addictive behaviors like food, sleep, sex, work without rest (workaholic), alcohol, drugs, and related substances and forms of addiction (anger, inferiority or superiority complex, phobias, the list continues).

Addiction is no respecter of persons. Like the "culture of silence" and domestic violence, it can affect and infect every member of the family, school, social club, community, or country. Both the addicted and free member of society need help, respectively.

We need resource materials to help the liberated integrate into the society and stay liberated, while helping others still being held captive by a higher power outside of themselves. This transitional period could be challenging if not well handled. Nothing is more frustrating than wanting to help but unable due to the complexities of the problem, and lack of adequate human and materials resources.

Horatio Gates Spafford

Horatio Gates Spafford (October 20, 1828, New York- October 16, 1888, Jerusalem) was a prominent American lawyer, best known for penning the Christian hymn *"It Is Well With My Soul,"* following a family tragedy in which four of his daughters died. Horatio was a wealthy and devout lawyer, a Presbyterian church elder, and a notable property owner in Chicago. He lost his 2-year-old son, then came the great Chicago fire in 1871 that started on Sunday, October 8- Tuesday, October 10, 1871, consequently consumed all his buildings. He and wife, Anna, and four daughters (Annie, Maggie, Bessie, and Tanetta) decided to go on vacation in Europe, but a zoning meeting delayed him. His wife and four daughters traveled ahead boarded the ship, SS Ville du Havre, which was a French iron steamship that operated round trips between the northern coast of France and New York.

On November 22, 1873, their ship collided with the Scottish three-mastered iron clipper, Loch Earn and sank in twelve minutes with the loss of 226 lives. Only 61 passengers and 26 crew members survived. Anna sent a telegram to Horatio in Chicago, which read "Saved alone what shall I do?" As he sailed past the spot where he lost all four daughters, Horatio wrote the hymn:

When peace like a river, attendeth my way,

When sorrows like sea billows roll,

What my lot, thou hast taught me to say,

It is well, it is well, with my soul.

Some Personalities Who Went From Misery To Ministry

In another development, according to Wikipedia, the free Encyclopedia, after the tragedy, on February 11, 1880, their son, Horatio Goertner Spafford, died of scarlet fever at the age of three (3). Their "new" daughters after the tragedy were Bertha Hedges Spafford (born on March 24, 1878) and Grace Spafford (born on January 18, 1881. Their Presbyterian Church regarded their tragedy as divine punishment. They finally found the American Colony in Jerusalem. The community grew over the years.

Visiting Chicago in 1894, Anna Spafford contacted Olaf Henrik Larsson, the leader of the Swedish Evangelical Church. Inspired by Anna's words and full of messianic fervor, the Swedes from Chicago decided to join Anna on her trip back to Jerusalem. Larsson also exhorted his relations and friends in Nas, Sweden, to go immediately to Jerusalem. Thus, thirty-eight (38) adults and seventeen (17) children sold all their possessions and set off for the Holy Land to join the Colony, arriving there in July 1896.

The Colony, now numbering 150, moved to the large house of a wealthy Arab landowner outside the city walls. The vast land attached to the house was quickly used for the Colony's support. Frequent visitors from Europe and America used part of the building as a hostel. A small farm developed with cows and pigs, a butchery, a dairy, a bakery, a carpenter's shop, and a smithy. The American Colony Store provided additional support through the sale of images, souvenirs, artifacts and archaeological objects worldwide.

The American Colony at Work: When the Swedes, who eventually joined the American Colony, left for Jerusalem, they brought their carpentry tools, hand looms, knitting machines and many farm implements with them. Colony members also collected specimens of the flowers mentioned in the Bible (Isa. 28:23, Prov. 31:13, 1 Kings 7:26, and Matt. 2:10, 11) that they pressed and pasted on cards and in albums and books to sell to tourists and pilgrims. Members fashioned this memorial for Horatio when he died in 1888, at the age of sixty.

Photographic Department of the American Colony: In 1898, the Colony bought an old camera to document the visit of Kaiser Wilhelm II of Germany to Jerusalem. From this humble beginning, the photographic studio became world famous for the thousands of images it produced of the Holy Land and the Middle East. Among the Colony members who worked in the studio were Lewis Larsson, Lars Lind, and John Whiting.

The American Colony Touched Lives: The American Colony near Jerusalem touched so many lives as they established orphanages and children's center. They also trained nurses for help to disaster victims during the locust plague in Europe. They were very helpful with relief work and supplies during World War 1 and beyond.

The Point of Connection With Book Title: In relation to the book title, Anna and Horatio Spafford come to us in the discussion as "wounded soldiers," but they did not allow their predicament to suppress their divine call and vision, so they persisted and strove together as Christian couple, who had experienced too much pain to mention. The story of the American Colony in Jerusalem and the huge impact they made and continue to make even years after their departure to be with the Lord in Heaven. Indeed, their Ministry is Where their Misery Was. Today during the most painful human losses, the hymn, *"It Is Well with My Soul"* is sung to comfort many.

John Newton

John Newton's story like that of Horatio Spafford is very relevant to the book title. Newton was born in 1725, but his mother died before his 7th birthday (the first misery to resonate with all whose parents passed away in the early years of their lives). He had a stern father who took him to sea at age eleven, too young for sea adventures on the boisterous seas. John Newton, therefore, was an alcoholic and a reckless youth. The British Navy noticed John Newton and consequently recruited him. His performance was impressive, till he attempted to desert the noble profession. He was caught and disciplined with eight dozen (ninety-six) lashes and reduced to an ordinary seaman. During a horrible storm off the coast of Ireland, their ship faced an imminent danger of capsizing. Amazingly in that turbulence, the cargo shifted and filled a hole in the ship's hull and finally drifted them to safety. This phenomenal experience was the beginning of his personal encounter with the Lord Jesus Christ. It was the starting point of his conversion experience that later impacted many lives positively.

Newton was a former slave master, a British sailor, and finally, an Anglican clergy who died at age 82. His past rough life and his conversion story and experiences gave birth to the hymn "Amazing Grace" which soothes and comforts the heart in the most disastrous moment. "Amazing Grace" was sung by President Barrack Obama during the eulogy for Reverend Clementa Pinckney, who was killed in the shooting at Charleston's Church. It has been widely acknowledged as one of the most powerful moments of his presidency. I produce below for the reader's careful reflection on the words and the melody.

*1. Amazing grace! How sweet the sound
That saved a wretch like me!
I once was lost, but now am found;
Was blind, but now I see.*

*2. Twas grace that taught my heart to fear,
And grace my fears relieved;
How precious did that grace appear
The hour I first believed.*

*3. Through many dangers, toils and snares,
I have already come;
'Tis grace hath brought me safe thus far,
And grace will lead me home.*

*4. The Lord has promised good to me,
His Word my hope secures;
He will my Shield and Portion be,
As long as life endures.*

*5. Yea, when this flesh and heart shall fail,
And mortal life shall cease,
I shall possess, within the veil,
A life of joy and peace.*

*6. The earth shall soon dissolve like snow,
The sun forbear to shine;
But God, who called me here below,
Will be forever mine.*

*7. When we've been there ten thousand years,
Bright shining as the sun,
We've no less days to sing God's praise
Than when we'd first begun.*

The Point of Connection With Book Title

John Newton's personal encounter with the Lord Jesus Christ led to his conversion, which made him abandon the hitherto prosperous and lucrative slave trade. Committed to the genuineness of his conversion, he became a stalwart and an advocate for the abolition of the slave trade in Britain. According to Wikipedia, the free encyclopedia, Newton was an Anglican clergyman and former slave-ship master. It took him a long time to speak out against the slave trade, but he had an influence on many evangelical Christians, notably William Wilberforce. He collaborated with William Cowper to produce a volume of hymns, including 'Amazing Grace.' So, popular was his preaching, which the church could not accommodate all those who flocked to hear him.

Newton began to regret his involvement in the slave trade deeply. After he had become Rector of St. Mary Woolnoth, in London in 1779, his advice was sought by many influential figures in Georgian society, among them the young M.P., William Wilberforce. Wilberforce was contemplating leaving politics for the ministry. Newton encouraged him to stay in Parliament and "serve God where he was." Wilberforce took his advice and spent the rest of his life working towards the abolition of slavery. In 1787, Newton wrote a tract supporting the campaign, 'Thoughts upon the African Slave Trade.' Thus, his "Ministry became Where His Misery Was."

Reflection on the Genesis of Your Ministry

The reader's sober reflection will lead to the source of his or her ministry. In other words, the motivating factors that gave birth to your ministry. Ministry in this context applies to God's divine calling on one's life (ordination/profession/career/"secular ministry"). With most people, the rough and challenging times in the past led them to do what they do today.

The book title applies to many in ministry, but unfortunately, some are not able to establish the link between their past misery and present ministry. The more you acknowledge and appreciate your humble beginnings, the more you become grateful and dependent on God. The more you realize your nothingness minus God, the humbler you are. The more compassionate you are for people, the more passionate you become in ministry as you serve God through the closest neighbor. A passionate response to the Great Commission (Matt. 28:16-20) will make our communities better than we are experiencing now. Gun violence in some cities in the US is on the increase, and I keep on asking myself, "where are the believers, and what are we doing? What are we doing with the power of God entrusted to us? Are we rather busy with other trivial things in the House of God to the neglect of the Great Commission? The command is Go Ye! And Not Come Ye! Neither is it, Stay Ye!"

CHAPTER 3

The Hidden Pain Gave Birth To Ministry

The Present Ministry is Traceable to Past Pain

With the majority of ministers, their present ministry is traceable to their past pain or the painful loss of a loved one. As mentioned earlier in this book and with some specific examples, the real uncontrollable pain with many addictions gave birth to their respective glorious ministries today. Jentezen Franklin today openly talks about his past pain and the feeling of insufficiency, insecurity, and fear. Today he champions, and advocates for all to be bold in whatever God has called each of us to accomplish in this world before we leave for heaven. His book, "Fear Fighters," is one of the books extensively being advertised by TBN. Joel Osteen, Pastor of Lakewood Church in Houston, Texas, USA, in another development, speaks of how for many years he worked for his father (John Hillery Osteen was the founder and first pastor of Lakewood Church) from behind the scenes with television production and editing. However, at the appointed time he came to the forefront when his father went to be with the Lord some years ago, (January 23, 1999). Today Joel champions the crusade of hope with his favorite program "Night of Hope" and regular television preaching. A Catholic priest once suffered from alcohol addiction, and after the power of the Holy Spirit liberated him, he began to minister to many alcohol addicts, until his death in Ghana a few months ago. Thus, his later life was more glorious than the former (His misery eventually became his ministry, too powerful, to touch other lives gloriously and diversely).

Whatever the devil meant for the worse, God can use it for the best to glorify himself. Regardless of the addiction, you may be in bondage to, do not hide in obscurity, but avail yourself for help, because once liberated, always liberated to help others. The life of Apostle Paul amplifies the point of emphasis here to encourage everyone. Paul boldly and confidently declared,

> "For I am the least of the apostles and do not deserve to be called an apostle, because I persecuted the church of God. By the grace of God I am what I am, and his grace to me was not without effect. No, I worked harder than all of them- yet not I, but the grace of God that was with me - (1 Cor. 15:9-10, NIV).

My Passion for Ministry is Advocacy and Bridge Building

As ministers, we must boldly admit the fact that our past pains and wounds, which are now healed should propel us in our ministry to help others. We have become "wounded healers." The book, the "Wounded Healer" by Henri Nouwen, speaks more on this very point. Where were you wounded in the past and now healed by divine grace? If indeed healed, then you are being sent out to the nations as a wounded healer with the message of the cross and hope to our dying world, which desperately seeks for freedom and peace outside the Prince of Peace himself. Jesus emphatically is the peace the world needs "...the Prince of Peace (Isa. 9:6). Jesus among his many duties, was an advocate for freedom and proclaimer of the Kingdom of heaven (... And saying, the time is fulfilled, and the kingdom of God is at hand: repent ye, and believe the gospel- Mark 11:15, KJV). He was also a "bridge builder" who invited all to walk on his completed beautiful bridge to heaven. He recommends same to all his followers reading this book today.

The Silent Majority Must Also Be Heard

In the ancient Jewish culture and during the days of Jesus, women and children were the silent majority as confirmed in the feeding of the five thousand, which excluded women and children (Matt. 14:21). Today, the same "culture of neglect" prevails in many cultures and traditions. In traditional Africa/Ghana, and in some contemporary societies, even in the 21st century, women and children are not heard for reasons best known to their leaders. With some, it is a systemic problem that has evolved over the years and entrenched by a patriarchal male-dominated society. Elizabeth Schussler Fiorenza (born 17 April 1938, Cenad), is a Romanian –born German, Roman Catholic feminist theologian, who is currently the Krister Stendahl Professor of Divinity at Harvard Divinity School, makes a case with the feeding of the five thousand and says that, the point of amplification or emphasis is rather the silent majority, being women and children.

This book among others seeks to empower the reader who suffered a similar neglect or rejection in the past, to come to terms and admit the inhumanness of the system, and further speak for the silent majority. In some churches and religious institutions of today, women and children are not given equal attention, which is rather unfortunate. All things being equal, women spend more time with the kids at home than most men. Again, since the family is the domestic church and the essential building block of society, it stands to reason that women and children must be deeply involved in any decision-making process, which affects the micro and macro community.

Many Are Dying in their Homes

The preceding paragraph has already thrown more light on this sub-heading. Most of the community is sidetracked by their cultural and traditional landscape. Even though they have voices, they cannot speak out to express their minds on pertinent, pressing, and critical issues that affect the community. The continued culture of silence has rendered many mentally redundant and incapable to productively use their brains because they have been denied the chances to meaningfully express their mind and contribute to any ongoing critical discussion, even matters that affect them.

My educational experiences in Ghana and the US reveal that the woman is as intelligent as the man. Again, no one should underrate the thinking power of little children. From Friday,

September 2- Sunday, September 4, 2016, I was in Worcester, Massachusetts, for the Council of Brong Ahafo Associations of North America (COBAANA) Convention. As a resource speaker at the Convention, I displayed some of my books and spoke about them. Amazingly, most of the interesting and critical-thinking questions were asked by the children. It was unbelievable! I know they need guidance, parental supervision, and counsel from time to time. We must not exclude and ignore them. As parents and guardians, we must intentionally create opportunities for them to express their mind and develop their critical thinking process. We must periodically engage them in meaningful discussions on societal issues that affect everyday life.

The time for liberation is now. Let us open the door wide and allow our women and children to freely speak out and express their views on critical issues that affect our communities. We must promote this initiative beginning from our homes, the religious and secular circles.

The Time to "Unveil" the Curtain for Transparency is Now

The human society, on the whole, has not benefited much because of the "hidden agenda" by some leaders at all levels. Transparency is not a friendly word to some group of people. Therefore, to advocate for transparency is to step on the toes of some powerful giants, who strongly feel that they are ordained to rule, dominate and control others and every available resource. Any attempt to talk about fairness and level playing field for all attracts hatred and name-calling. Transparency is key to any meaningful development.

Any considerate and servant leader at heart invites others to the "round table conference" for critical discussion that will positively impact the lives of others. This kind of compassionate leader thinks about the next generation, whereas most politicians think more about the next elections as soon as they assume office. What is your leadership style? Do you delegate power to others and follow up? Do you have any dream/vision for your people? What is your "hidden agenda" that is unknown to even your close associates?

The Bible admonishes us that two are better than one. This biblical principle applies to almost all human endeavors. You cannot know it all as a leader. Hear the alternative views and through the inspiration of the Holy Spirit, discern the best for your administration and the people you lead.

> "Two are better than one, because they have a good return for their labor. If either of them falls down, one can help the other up. But pity anyone who falls and has no one to help them up" (Eccl. 4:9-10, NIV).

CHAPTER 4

The "Culture Of Silence" Must End

The Culture Itself Imprisons the Individual

The "culture of silence" has stifled progress indeed and further militated against freedom. In my second book, I discussed the "culture of silence" and domestic violence and family life in the Brong Ahafo region of Ghana. The "culture of silence" as a matter of fact, prevails and persists almost at every aspect of societal life. You name it- families, communities, churches, schools, social clubs and associations, and nations. To talk about it in politics, especially, in Africa, will be an "exaggerated adventure." In otherwise, it is a standard feature in African politics just as it is in other countries. Lack of freedom of expression is tantamount to "imprisonment" of the citizenry. Get a copy of my book on the "culture of silence" to learn more about some hidden truths in some cultures in Africa. As much as the African culture has its positive side, the downside can be dangerous and hostile to human and societal development. For sure, the "culture of silence" must end with the 21st century so that we can hand over to the next generation a better society with sound cultural values of justice, fairness, equality, transparency, productivity, and accountability. We must not systemically perpetuate the dysfunctional culture of silence and abuse of morality we inherited. If we do, posterity will speak out against us.

The Church Must Take the Lead

I am always optimistic about the saving and the transforming power of the Gospel of Jesus Christ, entrusted to the Church (The Body of Christ) in every country, and therefore, look up to the pastors and leaders to equip the congregation to infuse the needed changes in every starter of the society.

> **"For I am not ashamed of this Good News about Christ. It is the power of God at work, saving everyone who believes--the Jew first and also the Gentile" (Rom. 1:16, NLT).**
>
> **"And he gave the apostles, the prophets, the evangelists, the shepherds and teachers, to equip the saints for the work of ministry, for building up the body of Christ" (Eph. 4:12-13, ESV).**

The book of the Acts of the Apostles, which others call the Acts of the Holy Spirit, is such a transforming book in the Bible. By my evangelistic nature, I love it because of its transforming power in the lives of individuals and the society. In it, fearful disciples after waiting and receiving the promise of the Father in Acts 1:8, and Acts 2:1-5, boldly proclaimed the Word of God with power and authority.

> "But you will receive power when the Holy Spirit comes upon you. And you will be my witnesses, telling people about me everywhere--in Jerusalem, throughout Judea, in Samaria, and to the ends of the earth" (Acts 1:8, NLT).

The timid Apostle Peter stood up and ministered boldly on the Day of Pentecost at the first New Testament crusade, and three thousand (3,000) souls responded to his message. They were pricked in their hearts, responded to the Gospel of Christ and experienced a life of conversion.

> "Now when they heard this they were cut to the heart, and said to Peter and the rest of the apostles, "Brothers, what shall we do?" And Peter said to them, "Repent and be baptized every one of you in the name of Jesus Christ for the forgiveness of your sins, and you will receive the gift of the Holy Spirit. For the promise is for you and for your children and for all who are far off, everyone whom the Lord our God calls to himself. "And with many other words he bore witness and continued to exhort them, saying, "Save yourselves from this crooked generation." So those who received his word were baptized, and there were added that day about three thousand souls" (Acts 2:37-41, ESV).

Missionaries traveled to the remotest parts of Africa and built churches, established schools, built clinics and hospitals, and provided other social amenities, which opened the door to development, not only to the new converts to Christianity but all. I plead with the churches to consciously budget for holistic development (body, soul, and spirit) to cater for the total man.

Leadership to Embrace Critical Feedback

We must learn from our miseries to improve our present ministries, especially, as leaders shepherding God's people. When we spoke our piece of mind in the past, it attracted hatred and hostilities. Now that we are in leadership positions let us not repeat same mistakes but embrace critical feedback. The good and compassionate leader embraces critical-thinking and feedback to promote compassionate and abiding ministry.

To remember your past pain or misery in the context of this book is a determination to do better and improve the lives of others. It helps you to be more proactive and progressive in your ministry. One good leader makes a huge difference, and the converse is also true. You may have possibly criticized other leaders in the past and became very impatient and frustrated when your constructive suggestions were ignored and thrown overboard. Furthermore, you were branded as rebellious to leadership. Now that you are in the position of authority aim at doing something different to permeate a positive change in a larger spectrum. Let us remember that each of us is a leader in one form or the other. You are either a mother, father, guardian, foster parent, pastor, minister, elder, deacon, deaconess, class captain, leader, school prefect, teacher, professor, supervisor, coordinator, head of a department, union leader, CEO, the list continues. Change does not come accidentally. Bishop TD Jakes puts it better and says that **"success is intentional, no one wins the Olympics by accident."**

It is About Issues Not Personalities

Most of the leadership problems and conflicts we grapple with, come from the fact that some leaders cannot differentiate between issues and personalities (personal interest, uncomfortable to embrace alternative views/ ideas), and therefore, hold tightly to power, even at the detriment to the larger society. The good leader delegates and follows up with an eagle's eye to make sure that the task is accomplished excellently and in a timely fashion to benefit all. Anything that falls short of this runs the whole administrative/leadership machinery into preventable and avoidable problems. Lift the critical issues at stake and invite critical minds to brainstorm for critical-thinking outcomes. In such meetings, you do not have to destroy to build. In other words, do not attack the previous speaker or contributor to the discussion before you establish your point. Just say something like this, "I hear the speakers that went ahead of me, but I am also of the opinion that the issue on the floor should be like this." By this, you are adding to the discussion and whoever is the facilitator/moderator must be fast and smart enough to summarize the surfacing outcome for the deliberations to end peacefully and beneficially. One issue should not take all the time for the meeting. The 21st century calls for leaders in biblical times like Joseph in Egypt (Genesis chapters 37-44), Moses and the Israelites (Exodus chapters 3-14 and Numbers 11:16) Daniel in Babylon (Daniel chapters 2-5), and others.

Constructive Criticism Promotes Growth and Development

I believe Moses, Joseph, David, and Daniel had their leadership challenges and oppositions but they stood their ground to prevail. Efficient and proactive leaders set the stage right to receive critical feedback and criticisms. Under such friendly atmosphere, ideas, views, and suggestions flow uninterrupted like a waterfall. The one criticizing must equally provide alternatives to impact the discussion positively. Criticisms without alternative suggestions only amount to hatred for the sitting leader. The incumbent leader should not feel threatened when the sharp brains challenge his administration. As long as alternative views are provided, the good leader should embrace all such useful suggestions for intellectual, argumentative, and Holy Spirit-inspired analysis. The issues under discussion at the round table conference have nothing to do with age, seniority, family affiliation and connection, the one who has been in the establishment/institution for long, or the first to come, or the other. When the best brains are at work, the outcome promotes growth and development to benefit all.

A Lesson for Individuals, Families, Churches/Institutions, Communities, and Nations

Progress, promotion, and proactivity take the lead when people are humble enough to learn a lesson from an unpleasant/painful past. A lesson learned from the painful past gives way to "ministry." Ministry in this context is simply service to humanity. To achieve the progress, we are all craving for, calls for our willingness to learn from past mistakes, unpleasantness experiences, challenges, problems, and, being very willing to make amends to move to the next level.

The human factors always combine with the divine to bring about excellent results and outcomes to affect and infect human growth and development. Let us always strike a balance between human and divine factors. God has always been in partnership with people. Let us, therefore, consult, trust and depend on him in whatever we plan to do. We must equally remember that whatever we do must finally bring the desired glory and honor to God. (So whether you eat or drink or whatever you do, do it all for the glory of God- 1 Cor. 10:31, NIV).

CHAPTER 5

The Misery Cannot Persist

Speak to End Miseries in the Hearts of Many

As minsters of God, we should speak to alter the lives of our audience for better. No one intentionally invites trouble or pain for himself or herself. Circumstances and situations beyond our control unexpectedly catch up with us in life. For example, the sudden death of a loved one. The good news is that nothing takes our loving God by surprise so we can always take comfort and consolation in his ever-abiding love during such seasons of our lives.

The Bible, which is the spoken Word of God, has answers to all our human predicaments. The minister whose ministry was born out of past personal and painful experiences becomes a blessing to the hurting at this trying periods. Hurting people are worried, confused, angry, and are easily irritated. It takes an anointed man or woman of God to comfort the hurting, using God's Word. Let us remember that there are much pain and hostility in our world today because "hurting people hurt others." It is as simple as that. Some do not do it intentionally by way of retaliation. Not at all. The pain disorganizes and disorientates them so much that their very behavior becomes a nuisance to all those around them. They carry the "emotional, painful baggage" wherever they go.

Being around them is unpleasant. They even bring their hurts to church and other sacrilegious places. They inadvertently extend it to the innocent doctors and nurses who take care of them when they are sick, and even to their pastors and church leaders. They give a piece of it to everyone who gets closer to them. Their spouses will need extraordinary grace and a big heart to embrace and contain their attitude. The minister must admit, highlight his or her misery, and amplify the point of conversion and liberation because God has purposefully given you this unique ministry to help others.

One minister I highly respect and admire greatly is Pastor Robert Morris of the Gateway Church, Dallas, Fort Worth, Texas, who openly shares his past immoral life and how the Holy Spirit set him free. His present ministry is where his misery was. The Lord has blessed his ministry so much that he turns around to bless others by way of giving to support the needy globally in obedience to the following scripture verses:

> **1. I have shewed you all things, how that so laboring ye ought to support the weak and to remember the words of the Lord**

Jesus, how he said, it is more blessed to give than to receive (Acts 20:35, KJV).

2. He that hath pity upon the poor lendeth unto the Lord, and that which he hath given will he pay him again (Prov. 19:17, KJV).

3. For I was hungry, and ye gave me meat: I was thirsty, and ye gave me drink: I was a stranger, and ye took me in... (Matt. 25:35-40, KJV).

4. Bear ye one another's burdens, and so fulfil the law of Christ (Gal. 6:2, KJV).

5. For the poor, shall never cease out of the land: therefore, I command thee, saying thou shall open thine hand wide unto thy brother, to thy poor, and to thy needy, in thy land (Deut. 15:11, KJV).

6. Give to him that asketh thee, and from him, that would borrow of thee turn not thou away (Matt. 5:42, KJV).

7. He that oppresseth the poor reproacheth his Maker: but he that honoureth him hath mercy on the poor (Prov. 14:31, KJV).

8. Give, and it shall be given unto you; good measure, pressed down, and shaken together, and running over, shall men give into your bosom. For with the same measure that ye mete withal, it shall be measured to you again (Luke 6:38, KJV).

9. Sell that ye have, and give alms; provide yourselves bags which wax not old, a treasure in the heavens that faileth not, where no thief approacheth, neither moth corrupteth... (Luke 12: 33-34, KJV).

10. He that hath a bountiful eye shall be blessed; for he giveth of his bread to the poor (Prov. 22:9, KJV).

11. He that giveth unto the poor shall not lack: but he that hideth his eyes shall have many a curse (Prov. 28:27, KJV).

12. Beloved, let us love one another: for love is of God; and every one that loveth is born of God, and knoweth God... (1 John 4:7-8, KJV).

13. Deliver the poor and needy: rid[them]out of the hand of the wicked (Ps. 82:4, KJV).

14. However, to do good and to communicate forget not: for with such sacrifices God is well pleased (Heb. 13:16, KJV).

15. For thou hast been a strength to the poor, a strength to the needy in his distress, a refuge from the storm, a shadow from the heat, when the blast of the terrible ones [is] as a storm [against] the wall (Isa. 25:4).

16. Moreover, the second [is] like, [namely] this, thou shall love thy neighbour as thyself. There is none other commandment greater than these (Mark 12:31, KJV).

17. Heal the sick, cleanse the lepers, raise the dead, cast out devils: freely ye have received, freely give (Matt. 10:8, KJV).

The Bible references above are relevant to the book title because they invite the author and reader to do something to help the needy person/neighbor. We were once in need of them (misery), and the act of going to serve them (Ministry) is a divine command and mandate upon our lives. So, we respond humbly in obedience.

Many Die Silently on Daily Basis Out of Misery

Most people believed that emotional pain kills faster than physical pain. This belief is vague and unsubstantiated with scientific proof, but I am tempted to think that it is correct because of my many years of experience as a professional staff chaplain at the University of Chicago Medical Center. The Spiritual Care Department is an integral part of the care team and with effective collaboration, chaplains complement and supplement the work of the medical doctors and the other members of the care team. Whenever the chaplains identify either an emotional or spiritual problem, the physical or medical becomes easier to diagnose and treat. This therapy is what I refer to as "holistic healing" in my first book, Integral Pastoral Care in Ghana: Proposals for Healing in the Asante Context.

Ministers of the gospel are encouraged to touch on the core issues facing their congregation. I mean the disturbing and shameful things going on in their lives, which many just refuse to talk about. I recommend that all churches should have a "professional counseling" department or ministry to meet such needs. Many people have been in various churches for years, but they have not had the trust to confide in their pastors or ministers to genuinely share their challenges so that they can be ministered to and experience liberation. No longer can we afford to allow church members and community members to die silently on a daily basis out of misery.

Society Will Not Forgive Those Who Compromise

Picking on my last sentence above, I am of the view that all must be watchful to keep an eagle's eye on our close family members and neighbors. The "culture of silence" has persisted for far too long in our communities to destroy precious lives. The perpetrator, the victim, and bystanders are the three key individuals involved in any violence or crime committed. My message in this paragraph is more for the bystanders, the onlookers, the compromisers. All victims must speak up for help, and all perpetrators must also do same. The offender needs help through counseling and prayer. It is more of behavior than spiritual attack. It is possible to come out of it in Jesus' name. It requires a mental shift to end the behavioral addiction and constant abuse and violence. You do not need the police to beat you up before you stop. Let us wake up to help family members and friends that are trapped in abusive relationships. Society will not forgive us if we compromise.

> "Therefore to him knoweth to do good, and doeth [it] not, to him it is sin" (James 4:17, KJV).

The Concerned Leader Thinks About the Next Generation

The pastor, minister, and leader takes the initiative to bring about change- a positive shift in the lives of the people who follow him or her. While serving as an interview panelist at the University of Chicago Medical Center (Spiritual Care Department), an interviewee once said something, which has stuck with me all these years. He said, "a leader without following is only taking a long walk." This remark by the interviewee means that every leader should have followers who respect and accept their counsel and instructions by heart. The followers do not only have to obey instructions but also to benefit from the leader's wisdom and improve their lives. The symbiotic relationship between the leader and the follower is a give-and-take affair for collective sanity and development.

While some political leaders only think about the next elections, the concerned leader thinks about the next generation regarding holistic progress- health, food, education, shelter, work ethics and employment, respect for rules and laws, civil and political responsibilities, spiritual growth, and concern for all. An efficient and visionary leader puts in place a workable system to affect and infect the present and next generations positively. Just acquaint yourself with these characteristics below about the great and caring leader:

1. Wisdom: Proverbs 8:15-By me (wisdom) kings reign and rulers make laws that are just. Proverbs 20:8- When a king sits on his throne to judge, he winnows out all evil with his eyes. All leaders must have God's wisdom. Jesus was filled with God's wisdom and grace (Luke 2:40). Wisdom is different from mere knowledge. The wise leader can see farther than others. His spiritual discernment is what sets him apart as God's leader. The church today is in dire need of godly wise leaders.

2. Integrity: *Proverbs 16:12- Kings detest wrongdoing, for a throne is established through righteousness. Proverbs 29:4- By justice, a king gives a country stability, but one who is greedy for bribes tears it down.* Personal integrity is demonstrated by who we are and what we do when no one is looking. In recent years, the Enron Corporation scandal left millions of Americans feeling very disturbed. However, there is one person within that infamous scandal that represent honesty and courage. Christian radio host Chuck Colson tells the true story of former Enron Vice President Sherron Watkins. Colson said, "While the whole Enron collapse seems to tarnish the reputation of nearly all of Enron's senior management, there is one notable exception. Her name is Sherron Watkins."

3. Love: *Proverbs 20:28- Love and faithfulness keep a king safe; through love, his throne is made secure.* How we love is more important than what we know or achieve. The Pharisees in Jesus' day were religious but unloving. People do not care how much you know until they know how much you care.

4. Seeks Good Advisers: *Proverbs 11:14- For lack of guidance a nation falls, but many advisers make victory sure. Proverbs 25:4- 5- Remove the dross from silver and out comes material for the* *silversmith; remove the wicked from the king's presence, and his throne will be established through righteousness.* Every effective leader needs advice and seeks help. The ability to listen to the discrete opinion of others is the mark of a great leader. In 1990, General Norman Schwarzkopf was Commander in Chief of U.S. Forces in Operation Desert Shield, undertaken to prevent Iraq from moving against Kuwait. During the days of the war, he assembled 765,000 troops from twenty –eight countries, hundreds of ships and thousands of planes and tanks. General Schwarzkopf called General Colin Powell, then Chairman of the Joint Chiefs of Staff, every evening on the telephone to discuss the events of the day. One day a news reporter asked, "Why?" Schwarzkopf answered, "He was the only person in the world who knew what I was trying to do. He listened to my ideas, helped me form strategies and exposed my errors in judgment –daily."

5. Self-Control: *Proverbs 28:15- Like a roaring lion or a charging bear is a wicked man ruling over helpless people.* The leader who cannot control himself will not be able to command the respect of those he leads.

6. Awareness of his Influence: *Proverbs 29:2- When the righteous thrive, people rejoice; when the wicked rule, people groan.* In almost every era, no country has been able to rise above its leaders. For better or worse, people become like those they follow (spiritually; it is also true. All things being equally, no member of the church or group can develop more than the senior pastor or leader as evidenced in my ministry over the years from Hwidiem through Kumasi-Ghana to Chicago).

7. Compassion: *Proverbs 29:14- If a king judges the poor with fairness, his throne will always be secure.* Jesus is the ultimate model of caring for the poor, the outcasts, and children. He was naturally drawn to the weak who needed an advocate. That is why James teaches us that pure religion is to look after orphans and widows in their distress.

Mary Clarke grew up in Beverly Hills during World War II. She was a teenage beauty, loved Hollywood and liked dancing with young soldiers. Mary dreamed of being rich, married, and raising a family with seven children. It all came to pass, but twenty-five years after, her marriage ended in a painful divorce. With her marriage over and her children grown, she began her second life by helping the less fortunate. In 1977, she was convinced that she found God's true purpose for her life. Mary Clarke became Sister Antonia and made La Mesa Prison, near Tijuana, Mexico, her permanent home. Since 1977, Sister Antonia has lived by choice in a ten-foot concrete cell at La Mesa. With no hot water and surrounded by murderers, thieves, and drug lords, she attends to their needs around the clock. She raises bail money, finds antibiotics, distributes eyeglasses and artificial teeth, counsels the suicidal and washes bodies for burial. "I live on the premises," she explains, "in case someone is stabbed in the middle of the night." La Mesa was built for 600 but holds 2,500 prisoners. Once during a raging prison riot, Sister Antonia, a 5'2" woman wearing a nun's habit, calmly strolled into the battle, ignoring the bullets and flying bottles and ordered everyone to stop. Amazingly, they did. A former inmate said, "No one else in the world could have done that. She has changed thousands of lives." "Love," says Sister

Antonia is what she offers everyone. "I am hard on crime, but not the criminal." Sister Antonia understands the power of compassion. Her ministry is where her misery was (painful divorce).

8. No Need for Public Approval: *Proverbs 29:25- Fear of man will prove to be a snare, but whoever trusts in the Lord is kept safe.* The greatest freedom is having nothing to prove and no one to impress. Servant leaders are more concerned about pleasing God than their popularity with others. The desire for honor among men makes trusting God almost impossible. The leader who has his eyes on receiving the praise of men is not focused on obeying and pleasing God.

9. Moderation: *Proverbs 31:4-5- It is not for kings to drink wine; not for rulers to crave beer; lest they drink and forget what the law decrees and deprive all the oppressed of their rights.* I have seen leaders who were such heavy drinkers that eventually, due to their lack of self-control, they lost their positions.

10. Submission to God: *Proverbs 21:1- A king's heart is in the hand of the Lord; he directs it like a watercourse wherever he pleases. Hebrews 10:5- When Christ entered the world he said, Here I am O Lord, I have come to do your will.* The ability and willingness to do the will of God in our personal life and leadership are the most important characteristics of a good leader? When a man or woman is submissive to God and his Holy Spirit, God will direct the person in the way he/she can glorify Him the best. Source: Discipleship Resource, Meet Paul and Peggy, What is Missing Inside? Bible Study Lesson Plans)-Wikipedia.

The Minister is God's Mouthpiece

God has always overseen his creation. He is in full control of affairs and has never changed. God is not moved by what we humans fear and panic about. The good news is that he has put in place whatever we need to know and do in his Word, the Bible. Jesus Christ is the answer to the escalating chaos in our world today. Jesus' final exhortation and command in the Great Commission invites every Christian to share the Gospels' Good News with those we meet in our daily walk. The more faithfully people respond to the Good News, the better our world will be, and the converse is also true. So, I encourage everyone reading this book to answer the call and preach the word to those that come your way. Responding to the call is the avenue to exercise the inherent authority and power of the Gospel of Christ committed to our trust as Christians. There is no neutrality in this divine assignment. It is imperative that we all get involved.

Certain cultures depict God as grandfather or grandmother, provider, and supplier of our basic and critical needs. Yes, this is true, even beyond that. He is Jehovah Jireh, God our provider, and our all in all. Just take a moment and reflect on these names of God in the Old Testament:

1. **El Shaddai** (Lord God Almighty)- Gen. 17:1; Gen. 28:3; Gen. 35:11; Gen. 43:14; and Gen. 48:3

2. **El Elyon** (The Most High God) - Gen. 14:18

3. **Adonai** (Lord, Master)-Gen. 15:2

4. **Yahweh** (Lord, Jehovah) - Gen. 2:4

5. **Jehovah Nissi** (The Lord My Banner) - Gen. 17:15

6. **Jehovah Raah** (The Lord My Shepherd) - Ps. 23; Gen. 49:24; and Ps. 80:1

7. **Jehovah Rapha** (The Lord That Heals)- Gen. 15:26; Jer. 30:17; Jer. 3:22; Isa. 30:26; Isa. 61:1

8. **Jehovah Shammah** (The Lord Is There) - Ezk. 48:35.

9. **Jehovah Tsidkenu** (The Lord Our Righteousness) - Jer. 23:6

10. **Jehovah Mekoddishkem** (The Lord Who Sanctifies You) -Exod. 31:13

11. **El Olam** (The Everlasting God) - Gen. 21:33

12. **Elohim** (God) - Gen. 1:1

13. **Qanna** (Jealous) - Exd. 29:5

14. **Jehovah Jireh** (The Lord Will Provide) - Gen. 22:14

15. **Jehovah Shalom** (The Lord Is Peace) - Jdg. 6:24

16. **Jehovah Sabaoth** (The Lord of Hosts) 1 Sam. 1:3; Ps. 24:9-10; Ps. 84:3; and Isa. 6:5

Source: Wikipedia, the free Encyclopedia.

God has always been on the throne (Hebrews 13:1- Jesus Christ is the same yesterday, today, and forever; your Kingdom is an everlasting Kingdom - (Psalm 145:13). The minister is God's mouthpiece to remind all about his agenda for humanity; and the Soon Coming of His Son, Jesus Christ.

This era of grace will soon end to usher in the soon and in-Coming King. (He has appointed a day to judge the world Acts 17:31; he bids all to come to repentance, today is the day of salvation - 2 Cor. 6:2; he is not delaying as some think but wants all to repent- 2 Pet. 3:9). The continued delay of his coming is attributable to the slow pace of evangelism today compared to what the first century Christians did in the Acts of the Apostle or what some referred to as Acts of the Holy Spirit.

We are admonished to preach the word in season and out of season. Preaching the word should be a lifestyle for the believer.

> "Preach the word of God. Be prepared, whether the time is favorable or not. Patiently correct, rebuke, and encourage your people with good teaching" (2 Tim. 4:2, NLT).

Just examine your life and share the Gospel from your misery to encourage someone today. The book title among others is also a response to the Great Commission because your ministry is where your misery was.

My Ministry Is Where My Misery Was

CHAPTER 6

A New Dawn Of Hope

A New Dawn of Hope is Here Now

Almost all ministers who preach "Hope Messages" have a background of hopelessness. They encountered the presence of God, and there was 360 degrees turn around, and therefore, they talk from personal experience with life. Their past emotional pain makes them understand, resonate, and sympathize with those who go through various degrees of painful periods. They have personally had the conversion experience. Anyone who genuinely and honestly professes Jesus as Lord and Savior never remains the same. I had the conversion experience myself on June 6, 1972, and so, I come to the discussion from a lived and transformative experience. There are many today who have everything - good health, excellent education, reputable and well respected paid job, good family life, live in a safe and comfortable house and home, respected and honored in the community, a leader in an enviable position, and others. However, sadly, they are missing the real person, Jesus Christ in their lives. To miss Jesus is a life of emptiness and on a journey of constant search. Saint Augustine establishes this point with an imagery and says "our lives are empty until they rest in Christ." To have Jesus, therefore, is to have the full life.

The continued prayer of Saint Monica of Hippo (AD 331-387), the mother of Saint Augustine, brought about the conversion of her wayward son and now a Saint. It is not accidental that you are reading this page now. It is a page of hope, and indeed a new dawn of hope to invite you to be in fellowship with the Lord Jesus Christ. Matthew 6:33 is still valid, accurate, and authenticated:

> "Seek ye first the Kingdom of God and his righteousness and all these (physical and temporary properties and things as enumerated above) shall be added unto you as well."

Injustices and Myriads of Abuses Among Humanity Must Cease

The Holy Spirit announces a complete "cease fire" in this chapter. The various forms of injustice, lawlessness, violence, and gang activities are perpetrated against one another and for that matter, against God. God abhors sinful behaviors, and therefore, a sin committed against a neighbor is a sin against God. The Bible lists some of these sins as:

> "....Adultery, fornication, uncleanness, lasciviousness, idolatry, witchcraft, hatred, variance, emulations, wrath, strife, seditions,

heresies, envyings, murders, drunkenness, revellings, and such like: of the which I tell you before, as I have also told you in time past, that they which do such things shall not inherit the kingdom of God" (Gal. 5:19-21).

Paul again in the book of Romans lists another batch of sins, behaviors, habits, and attitudes and says that:

> "The wrath of God is being revealed from heaven against all the godlessness and wickedness of people, who suppress the truth by their wickedness...For though they knew God; they neither glorified him as God nor gave thanks to him, but their thinking became futile, and their foolish hearts were darkened. Although they claimed to be wise, they became fools and exchanged the glory of the immortal God for images made to look like a mortal human being and birds and animals and reptiles. Because of this, God gave them over to shameful lusts (Rom. 1:18-26, NIV).

Matthew continues with his list of sins and says that:

> "For out of the heart come evil thoughts –murder, adultery, sexual immorality, theft, false, testimony, slander. These are what defile a person; but eating with unwashed hands does not defile them" (Matt. 15:19-20, NIV).

The other open abuses are leaders who embezzle public funds and consequently innocent citizens suffer. Some patients in public health centers sleep on bare floors in some countries in Africa and elsewhere in the 21st century. Some children attend schools under trees; politicians tell lies to win elections (capitalizing on the ignorance of the citizenry); public and civil servants extort money before discharging their official duties, and some church leaders, unfortunately, abuse their members diversely. All these injustices and immoral behaviors should cease because they are a violation against humanity, and for that matter, against God.

The Holy Spirit in this scripture is reminding us of the best way-of-life to promote communal living. The Fruit of the Spirit is a biblical term that sums up nine attributes of the Christian life according to Paul in his Letter to the Galatians.

> "But the fruit of the Spirit is love, joy, peace, forbearance, kindness, goodness, faithfulness, gentleness, and self-control" (Gal: 5:22-23, NIV).

These attributes of the Kingdom of God at our disposal promote safe and harmonious living, togetherness, concern and care for another, progress, development, and holistic advancement in any family, community, church, association, institution, or nation.

The Loving Father Cares

The love of God is great, everlasting, unconditional, and beyond human comprehension. Since the fall of man in the Garden of Eden (Gen. 3), God continues to reconcile humanity to himself. The love of God is demonstrated by the death of Christ on the Calvary Cross. Apostle Paul confirms it and says that:

> But God commandeth his love toward us, in that, while we were yet sinners, Christ died for us (Rom. 5:8, KJV).

About the book title and the key issues raised so far, even during one's misery, the love of God manifests to prepare the individual for ministry. Nothing goes wasted in the loving hands of our God. Many encounter the love of God in their most awkward seasons- serving a jail term in prison, a soldier on the battlefield, a patient on the hospital bed, during a fatal accident, job loss, bereavement, examination failure, divorce, and others. It is unthinkable to talk about the love of God in painful situations like those listed above, but it is true. It is deeply experiential and nothing superficial. It is hard to talk about it from outside. You should be there to know, feel, and understand it as described by this scripture.

> "God comforts us so that we can comfort those in any trouble" (2 Cor. 1:4).

A Christian sister lost the husband and was so much embraced in the love of Christ that she experienced great divine support, which made it difficult for her to cry. This bereavement was in Ghana. By culture, the wife is supposed to wail, cry, scream, and beat herself up and down in sorrow. The deceased husband's family could not just understand, and therefore, concluded that she bewitched and killed her husband. It took a lot of energy and effort by the pastors and church leaders in the community to explain and defend the innocent Christian sister who was basking in the love of God.

May God extend same love to you now even as you read this page. Just pause and repeat this prayer after me: "Lord Jesus, I admit that I am a sinner, and have gone my ways. Today, I accept your love and confess you as my Lord and Savior. Come into my heart, and take control/charge of my whole life henceforth. I hand over the key of my life to you today. Take me, and make me your beloved child. Amen." Let us love and carry each other's burden. Let us love people and not things.

All Join Forces to Fight "Culture of Silence," Domestic Violence, and Injustices/Abuses

Lord Acton, an English Catholic historian, politician, and writer, once said that what concerns all must be decided by all. He also said that Power tends to corrupt, and absolute power corrupts absolutely. On freedom, he said that liberty becomes a question of morals more than of politics. Liberty in his view is the harmony between the will and the law. He critically studied human society and made certain truthful pronouncements. For example, he says that "the science of politics is the one science that is deposited by the streams of history, like the grains of gold in the sand of a river; and the knowledge of the past, the record of truths revealed by experience, is eminently practical, as an instrument of action and a power that goes to making the future." Acton contributes to wisdom and says further that, "the long-term versus the short-term argument is one used by losers." Finally, he says that "there is not a soul who does not have to beg alms of another, either a smile, a handshake, or fond eye; A wise person does at once, what a fool does at last. Both do the same thing; only at different times."

Pulling from the wisdom sayings of Lord Acton above, my message to the reader is simple. Let us wake up to our collective responsibilities as fellows in the same ship (fellowship) on the deep blue stormy sea. A concerted effort will enable us to sail ashore safely (in unity lies strength; United we stand, divided we fall). Divisive spirit only divides and separates us from one another. Dr. Martin Luther King, Jr. tells us that hatred only begets hatred, and violence begets violence. Whatever we need to do today to rescue our lives must be done now and not tomorrow. This is our generation, and we must all add to it, to make it better than before, before we hand over to the next generation. With this as our goal, we will break the "culture of silence" with its attendant problems of domestic violence, injustices of all forms and shapes, and the many cases of abuse in our families, communities, churches, schools, institutions, and countries.

Identify and Address the Misery in Ministry Intentionally

I employ all ministers to boldly identify and address the misery component of their respective ministries to benefit those who are still hiding in their closets of addictions, abuses, and domestic violence. If we have been truly redeemed, then let us say so to glorify God, and liberate others. God saved us to save others. Therefore, in our seasons of distress and discomfort, He comforts us.

> "He comforts us so that we can comfort those in any trouble" (2 Cor. 1:4).

I have already mentioned Pastor Robert Morris, who is an excellent example of my book title and his passionate message to the reader.

The "Heaven Call" Demands Accountability to Oneself, Others, and God

No one lives on an island alone; you need me, and I also need you. We need one another to function efficiently in ministry and life. Our relationship is paramount to succeed in ministry and life. You should not wallow in your misery alone. Speak up, share your burdens to receive help. Paul tells you to carry one another's burdens, and in this way, you will fulfill the law of Christ (Gal. 6:2, NIV). Both relationships, vertical (with divinity) and horizontal (with neighbors) is imperative for a meaningful and hopeful living. The good news is that if the vertical is fully in place through prayer, the Word, and holy living, the horizontal follows and flows naturally without a struggle.

Because the Holy Spirit lives the life of God through you - a life of credible witness, honesty, care, concern and respect for others becomes your greatest motivation in your relationship with others. Consequently, your ultimate desire becomes how to esteem others more than yourself (Phil. 2:3). As a Christian, whatever you do in this life is a "Call" and "Ministry" to serve God through serving people.

Calling or Ministry is of two types- "ordained ministry or the fivefold ministry revealed in Eph. 4:11-12," (to serve as a pastor, apostle, prophet, evangelist, teacher and leader in church or ministry) and "ordinary ministry" (to serve through your career or profession as a marketplace minister). Both ministries demand accountability and responsibility (honestly be yourself and do the best you can under all circumstances). Furthermore, seek to live peaceably with all (men, women, children, superiors, subordinates, juniors, employers, employees, and colleagues). Paul tells the believers in Rome and all of us that if it is possible, as much as it depends on you, live peaceably with all men (Rom. 12:18, NKJV). Our accountability to God should keep us watchful and vigilant 24/7 because of 1 Peter 4:17- For it is time for judgment to begin with God's household; and if it begins with us, what will the outcome be for those who do not obey the gospel of God?

CONCLUSION

Spirituality, Ministry, Misery, Compassion, And Passion

Deep Faith and Spirituality Confront Human Injustices

It takes a life of unwavering faith and persistent spirituality in God to confront human injustices in our world today. Dr. Martin Luther King, Jr. is a contemporary classic example as he boldly and passionately spoke about freedom for all in the United States of America. I have quoted him extensively in my first and second books, Integral Pastoral Care in Ghana: Proposals for Healing in the Asante Context, and The "Culture of Silence" and Domestic Violence. Dr. King says that "Our lives begin to end the day we become silent about things that matter." Touching on education, Dr. King says that "The function of education is to teach one to think intensively and critically… Intelligence plus character – that is the goal of true education."

Finally, he says, "**Nothing in the world is more dangerous than sincere ignorance and conscientious stupidity.**" Dr. King's racial activism and human rights advocacy were dependent on his deep faith and spirituality, as well as his character- the character of God in the life of the Christian is fearlessness, and ever ready to stand fully for the just cause regardless of whatever. Posterity will not honor and forgive anyone who compromises his or her faith, convictions, passion, and aspirations. Today, a major street is named after Dr. King in all the major US cities including Chicago. It is no wonder he once said: "**Love is the only force capable of transforming an enemy into a friend.**"

The Spirit of Courage and Boldness

The Word of God empowers all believers in 1 John 4:4- You, dear children are from God and have overcome them, because the one who is in you is greater than the one who is in the world. It takes courage and boldness to speak about one's past unpleasant life even though you have experienced a new life in Christ. As long as we cover up the misery story, others are not being encouraged to come out of their "imprisonment and addictions. My book seeks to empower all who have been dancing around their past stories of misery to proclaim it boldly. Own your misery to promote, project, and protect your ministry to the benefit of your audience. A concealed misery is not a liberated misery, and can likely trap you to fall one day. Speak up, ring the bell of freedom, and cry out to shame the devil. A hidden victory is not a celebrated triumph.

Contemporary Ministry Addresses Current Diverse Human Misery and Pain And Abuses

Contemporary ministration cannot act as if all is well with the human society. Before I proceed, I ask the question, "**who speaks for the voiceless?**" "**Who advocates for the needy and downtrodden in our communities?**" The "culture of silence" has muted almost everybody including men and women of God. Our best example of advocacy is Jesus himself. He boldly confronted the religious leaders of his day and spoke openly against their injustices and antisocial vices. He enters the temple to overturn the tables of the money changers.

The book at this point is stirring into your spirit the energy to do something new and more positive to affect and infect your community. You must address the current social disorders in your immediate environment, especially the many hidden miseries, pains, and the abuses people go through. Never assume that all is well with everybody in your church, group, school, and institution. You must push to get the reaction; stir to disturb the calm waters. An excellent preaching, sermon or homily identifies the human predicament and boldly addresses squarely the troubling societal issues and answers the question, and so, what next? What must I do as I move forward?

Compassion for People

A ministry born out of misery has compassion for people because the minister can easily identify with the suffering masses. The misery-oriented ministry never makes assumptions to conclude that all is well with everybody. To be effective in ministry, endeavor to see the individual in a three-dimensional perspective always. God desires that we are completely made whole; body, the physical, soul/mental and emotional, and spiritual, the hidden and unseen. Indeed, seeing through this point of view in ministry would bless and build people, conversely, will curse and destroy lives.

> "Now may the God of peace make you holy in every way, and may your whole spirit and soul and body be kept blameless until our Lord Jesus Christ comes again" (1 Thess. 5:23, NLT).

This three-dimensional perspective of ministry is the secret to building a genuine and abiding ministry. In line with the five-fold offices in Ephesians 4:11, the misery ministry should embark on a "spiritual division of labor" mission where "professionals" and gifted ministers handle what they can do efficiently, with excellence. The compassionate minister does not give room for any shoddy work in the house of God.

> "Now these are the gifts Christ gave to the church: the apostles, the prophets, the evangelists, and the pastors and teachers. Their responsibility is to equip God's people to do his work and build up the church, the body of Christ. This will continue until we all come to such unity in our faith and knowledge of God's Son that we will be mature in the Lord, measuring up to the full and complete standard of Christ" (Eph. 4:11-13, NLT).

Passion for Ministry

The compassion for people leads to passionate ministry. The passion and the burden become so pronounced that you just cannot live without doing it. The passion for souls becomes your number one priority and concern. The ministry of Apostle Paul readily comes to mind at this juncture. Without mincing words, Paul chronologically lists the dangers, struggles, and challenges he went through during his missionary journeys and passionately ends with an account of one of them on the note that "…Besides everything else, I face daily the pressure / burden of my concern for all churches" - (2 Cor. 11:28, NIV).

A contemporary example will be helpful here. I listened to a TBN program on Wednesday, September 14, 2016, at a time when I was getting ready to conclude this book. The program was titled "Stronger with Clayton King." In his book "Stronger," Clayton explores what it means to see God's strength made perfect in our weakness. He unpacks the paradox of how the Christian life is centered on making Jesus becoming bigger and we becoming smaller. He attested to the fact that the hard times we face in life do not make us happy, but rather keep us humble and make us holy. Clayton tells how he lost nine (9) family members within a span of twelve (12) years (an average of one death every 16 months), how his mother and father died 18 months apart, and how he preached at his father's funeral on Father's Day.

He narrates how his loving father had a stroke and struggled through for one and half years and eventually died. He was on a ministry assignment in Toronto Canada when his mother died. In the heat of the critical emotional stress, he called his friend in South Carolina, who readily responded and shared how he also lost his mother at age twelve (12), and how the Lord pulled him through. Clayton too was pulled through by the grace of God, and today, he supports many who are bereaved. Another contributor to the same program by name Nate Dooley (is the student Pastor at Long Hollow Baptist Church, overseeing five campuses, outside of Nashville, TN) also shared a similar story on bereavement and how the God of peace and love sustained him.

Both Clayton and Nate are being used mightily in ministry to support the grieving and hurting because of their losses. I like what Clayton said, "Let adversity be your university." In other words, the brokenness, failure, and disappointments we go through should be our "university" to learn more about ourselves, others, and God. Clayton concluded on the note that emotional understanding solidifies our faith and knowledge of God. It makes us more assured and certain of God's love. He further encourages all to "push through the seasons" as we seek mentors and counselors to companion us to understand our individual situations moment by moment.

According to Clayton, we should ask all the questions on our hearts because we have a big God who knows our pain and suffering. All contributors and questions asked at the program "Stronger with Clayton King" seemed to be saying that "My Ministry is Where My Misery Was." The program beautifully ended with the exhortation of Apostle Paul in Philippians 1:12-14 when he said:

> "...Moreover, I want you to know, my dear brothers and sisters, that everything that has happened to me here has helped to spread the Good News. For everyone here, including the whole palace guard, knows that I am in chains because of Christ. Moreover, because of my imprisonment, most of the believers here have gained confidence and boldly speak God's message without fear."

Prayer of Salvation

Acceptance, Rededication, Recommitment, And Refire!

Salvation: Prayer to accept Jesus Christ as Lord and Savior (ABCD of Salvation).

A = Admit in humility that you are a sinner by nature *(Romans 3:23)*.

B = Believe on the Lord Jesus Christ, and you shall be saved, and your household *(Acts 16:31)*.

C = Confess with your mouth the Lord Jesus and believe in your heart that God has raised him from the dead, you will be saved *(Rom. 10:9)*.

D = Dedicate your body to Christ henceforth as an instrument of righteousness *(Rom 12:1)*.

Repeat The Prayer After Me

Lord Jesus, I have heard your word today. I admit that I am a sinner.

I confess to you all my sins, known and unknown. Forgive me because I have greatly sinned against you. I accept you as my personal Lord and Savior. Come into my heart; take full control of my life. I hand over the key of my life to you. Take me and make me thy own henceforth. Amen!

If you prayed and believed the prayer, then John 1:12 is for you.

> **"...But as many as received him, to them gave he the power to become the sons of God, even to them that believe on his name."**

Rededication/Re-commitment

"Revive me, O Lord" (Ps. 119:156).

Please offer this Prayer of Re-dedication to the Lord:

"Revive Me, O Lord" (Ps. 119:156).

> "Restore unto me the joy of your salvation, and grant me a willing spirit, to sustain me" (Ps. 51:12).
>
> "Now the Lord is the Spirit, and where the Spirit of the Lord is, there is freedom" (2 Cor. 3:17).

Prayer By Author For Readers:

Gracious and everlasting God, through the inspiration and power of the Holy Spirit, I pray with the reader right now. Please, Lord, rekindle the individual's spirit with your love and peace and rejuvenate your child and restore your illumination and enlightenment to the yearning soul. In Jesus' Name. Amen!

My Ministry Is Where My Misery Was

Author's Profile

Dr. Gabriel Amoateng-Boahen was born to the Late Opanin Peter Kofi Amoateng (went to be with the Lord in February 1978) and the Late Maame Veronica Yaa Afrah (transitioned to Glory on March 19, 2013, thirty-five years after the death of my father) of Kintampo, Brong Ahafo, Ghana. He started school at the age of seven at the Bodom Presbyterian School and Effia Methodist Primary (near Effiakuma-Takoradi, the Port City). Gabriel returned to Kintampo in 1962 to continue his education at the Baffoe Local Authority and Middle Schools at Kintampo, where he was the Junior Prefect and Senior Prefect respectively (1962-1967; Gabriel's class was the first batch for the new school).

In 1967, Gabriel passed the Common Entrance Examination and gained admission to the Obuasi Secondary Technical School (1967-1972). From 1972-1974, Gabriel successfully completed his Post-Secondary Teacher Training College at Berekum, Brong Ahafo, and was posted to Ahafo Kenyasi II Catholic Primary School. A few weeks later, he was transferred to Ahafo Hwidiem Catholic Primary School, where Gabriel taught from 1974-1984 (part of divine plan unfolding –Jer.29:11).

Gabriel studied privately and passed the Advanced Level Examination and gained admission to pursue his undergraduate studies at the University of Science and Technology (now Kwame Nkrumah University of Science and Technology-KNUST) in Kumasi-Ghana from 1984-1987 and obtained his Bachelor of Arts in Social Sciences (final thesis "Comparative Study of Traditional and Church Marriages in the Brong Ahafo Region: A Case Study of the Hwidiem Traditional Area," UST, Kumasi-Ghana, 1987). From 1987-1989, Gabriel did the mandatory national service at the newly established Community Improvement Unit (CIU) at the Konongo District Office. Gabriel had a "desert experience" from 1990-1991 as he discerned God's plan for his life and also volunteered at the "infant" Maranatha Clinic (now Maranatha Hospital at Kwadaso/Asuoyeboa-Kumasi).

Gabriel was the Diocesan Development Coordinator for the Sunyani Catholic Diocese in 1991 and later became the headmaster for the St. Louis Junior Secondary School at Mbrom-Kumasi from 1992-1994. On May 6, 1995, he became the first-ever headmaster and co-founder of the Maranatha International School (now Maranatha Young Apostles) at Daban Panin-Kumasi. This school was established on sound Christian principles with the motto "Holistic Child Development" to demonstrate the harmonious interplay among hand, head, and heart (hand/body/physical, head/mind/soul/, and heart/the spirit of the human person- 1 Thess.5:23). Prov.9:10 and Prov. 22:6 were our key biblical verses, and both staff and students lived by the precepts of God's Word.

Gabriel arrived in New York on May 31, 2001, to pursue Clinical Pastoral Education (CPE) at the Hospital of Saint Raphael in New Haven, Connecticut, USA, to be trained as a

Chaplain, and thereafter proceeded to the Catholic Theological Union (CTU) in Chicago, Illinois, USA, for the Master of Arts in Pastoral Studies (MAPS) from 2002-2004 and the Ecumenical Doctor of Ministry degree from 2004-2007. Gabriel is a Certified Professional Chaplain (Retired) at the University of Chicago Medical Center and also the President and Founder of the Royal Diadem Pastoral Center in Chicago and Kumasi-Ghana.

Gabriel had a personal encounter and relationship with the Lord Jesus Christ on June 6, 1972, and ever since that time, has remained resolute and uncompromising with his Christian faith and has great passion for soul-winning. Gabriel has varied ministerial experiences. He was a member of the Scripture Union, Ghana (especially in the Ahafo and Sunyani areas), from 1974-1984; and he was the church secretary for the Holy Spirit Catholic Church at Ahafo Hwidiem. During that same period, he was the founder and first-ever secretary for the Ahafo Hwidiem Christian Fellowship and was also actively involved in the Council of Churches. Gabriel was the secretary of the first-ever Ghana Catholic School of Evangelization organized by the Germany and Malta teams and hosted by the Metropolitan Archdiocese of Kumasi-Ghana in 1992.

At the Catholic Charismatic Renewal front, Gabriel was a founding member of Mission 2000 (established on November 3, 1991), a Catholic Charismatic Renewal Prayer Group with focus on evangelizing Catholic adults and professionals. He is the current coordinator of the Charismatic Renewal at Our Lady of Sorrows Basilica at 3121 W. Jackson Boulevard in Chicago, and also a member of the Ghanaian Catholic

Charismatic Renewal –North America (G-CCR-NA) Leadership Coordinating Team (LCT) (appointed director for missions in June 2013 at the first-ever National Biennial Convention in Virginia). Gabriel is a founding member of the Ghanaian Catholic Community of Chicago and also the founder and coordinator of the Prayer Conference for the Catholic Community as well as the Christian Leaders for Tomorrow (CL4T) Prayer Conference- youth focused with Daniel 11:32b as its theme verse: "They that know their God shall be strong and do exploits." He is the "marriage counselor" for the local Catholic Community of Chicago and also for some Ghanaians in Chicago.

Dr. Gabriel is the Founder and President of Royal Diadem Pastoral Center. He is the Chaplain for the Brong Ahafo Association of Chicago and the keynote speaker at the Council of Brong Ahafo Associations of North America (COBAANA) in 2011; and he is also the Ombudsman for COBAANA. Gabriel has strong ecumenical inclination and is deeply involved in the activities of the Council of Ghanaian Churches in Chicago, where he is the current Vice President. Gabriel takes a lot of inspiration from Evangelist Dr. Billy Graham. He is Gabriel's "spiritual mentor" and has twice attended the Billy Graham Schools of Evangelism in Cincinnati, Ohio (2002), and Kansas City, Missouri (2004). Gabriel was at the Haggai Institute in Singapore in 2000 for the Advanced Leadership Training for Christian Leaders from Developing Countries.

He is a member of these professional associations: National Association of Catholic Chaplains (NACC), Association of Professional Chaplains (APC), Spiritual Direction International (SDI) and others. Gabriel was the representative for the University of Chicago Medical Center at the Kenwood-Hyde Park Interfaith Council (2010 - to May 31, 2015).

On March 27, 1977, Gabriel and Mrs. Agatha Amoateng-Boahen were joined together in holy matrimony at the Holy Spirit Catholic Church at Ahafo Hwidiem. They now live peacefully and happily with their eight children: Mrs. Veronica Amoateng Antwi; Rev. Sampson Amoateng; Rev. Mark Amoateng, MD; Rev. Daniel Amoateng; Rev. Brian Amoateng; Christabel Jessica Amoateng; Davina Amoateng; and Gabriel Amoateng Badu, Jr.

Conferences, Seminars, And Continuous Education

Ghanaian Catholic Charismatic Renewal- North America (G-CCR-NA), First-Ever Leadership Conference, Springfield, Virginia, USA, 2016.

Council of Brong Ahafo Associations of North America (COBAANA), Worcester, Massachusetts, USA, 2016

All Pastors and Leaders Conference (APALEC), Stratford Christian Center Church, Chicago, Illinois, USA, 2016.

Ghanaian Catholic Charismatic Renewal –North America (G-CCR-NA), Second Biennial Convention, Bronx, New York, USA, 2015.

All Pastors and Leaders Conference (APALEC), House of Miracles, Medina Estates, Accra-Ghana, 2015.

Ghana Catholic Charismatic Renewal (National Outreach Leaders) Conference, Adom Fie-Kumasi, 2015.

Council of Brong Ahafo Associations of North America (COBAANA) Convention, Bronx, New York, USA, 2014.

Diversity and Inclusion Competency, University of Chicago Medicine, Illinois, USA, Fall 2014.

Ghanaian Catholic Charismatic Renewal –North America (G-CCR-NA), First-Ever Biennial Convention, Falls Church, Virginia, USA, 2013.

Council of Brong Ahafo Associations of North America (COBAANA) Convention, Washington DC, USA, 2013.

All Pastors and Leaders Conference (APALEC), House of Miracles, Medina Estates, Accra-Ghana, 2013.

All Pastors and Leaders Conference (APALEC), Life Community Chapel, Kumasi-Ghana, 2013.

Council of Brong Ahafo Associations of North America (COBAANA) Convention, Columbus, Ohio, USA, 2012.

Council of Brong Ahafo Associations of North America (COBAANA) Convention, Chicago, Illinois, USA, 2011.

All Pastors and Leaders Conference (APALEC), House of Miracles, Medina Estates, Accra-Ghana, 2010.

Council of Brong Ahafo Associations of North America (COBAANA) Convention, Toronto, Canada, 2010.

Kwame Nkrumah University of Science and Technology (KNUST) Alumni National Conference, Chicago, Illinois, USA, 2010.

National Association of Catholic Chaplains' Conference, Columbus, Ohio, USA, 2006.

Benny Hinn Miracle Crusade, Milwaukee, Wisconsin, USA, 2004.

Billy Graham School of Evangelism, Kansas City, Missouri, USA, 2004.

Archdiocese of Chicago Charismatic Renewal Conference, Chicago, Illinois, USA, 2003.

Trained Volunteer Tutor at Laubach Literacy Action, Chicago, Illinois, USA, 2003.

Benny Hinn Miracle Crusade, Louisville, Kentucky, USA, 2002.

Billy Graham School of Evangelism, Cincinnati, Ohio, USA, 2002.

Investment in Africa Conference, Worcester, Massachusetts, USA, 2002.

Connecticut American Montessori Conference, Hartford, Connecticut, USA, 2002.

National Catholic Charismatic Renewal Conference, Scranton, Pennsylvania, USA, 2002.

National American Montessori Conference, Atlanta, Georgia, USA, 2001.

Advanced Leadership Training for Christian Leaders in Developing Countries, Singapore, Asia, 2000.

Catholic Charismatic Renewal Leaders' Conference, Kumasi-Ghana, 2000.

Berekum Training College Old Students Association (BETCOSA), Kumasi-Ghana, 2000.

First-Ever Ghana Catholic School of Evangelization by Germany and Malta Teams, Kumasi-Ghana, 1992.

Ghana Scripture Union /Christian Fellowship (Ecumenical) - Retreats, Crusades, Camp Meetings, and Conferences (Ahafo Hwidem, Goaso, Sunyani, and Kumasi), 1975-1988.

Author's Profile

Education

2004-2007: Catholic Theological Union (CTU), Chicago, Illinois, USA; Ecumenical Doctor of Ministry.

2005-2006: Claret Center, Chicago, Illinois, USA; Spiritual Direction International Internship.

2002-2004: Catholic Theological Union (CTU), Chicago, Illinois, USA; Master of Arts in Pastoral Studies (MAPS).

2001-2002: Clinical Pastoral Education (CPE) Residency, Saint Raphael Hospital, New Haven, Connecticut, USA.

1984-1987: Kwame Nkrumah University of Science and Technology (KNUST), Kumasi-Ghana, Bachelor of Arts (Social Sciences).

1972-1974: Berekum Post-Secondary Teacher Training College, Berekum, Brong Ahafo Region, Ghana.

1967-1972: Obuasi Secondary Technical (SECTECH) Obuasi, Ashanti Region, Ghana.

1960-1962: Kintampo Local Authority Primary and Middle Schools, Kintampo, Brong Ahafo Region, Ghana

1960-1962: Effia Methodist Primary School, Effia (Near Effiekuma, Takoradi Port City), Western Region, Ghana.

1959-1960: Bodom Presbyterian Primary School, Bodom-Nkoranza, Brong Ahafo Region, Ghana.

Employment History

2005-2015: Board Certified Professional Staff Chaplain, University of Chicago Medical Center, Chicago, Illinois, USA.

2014-2016: Ombudsman, Council of Brong Ahafo Associations of North America (COBAANA).

2013-2016: Missions Director, Ghanaian Catholic Charismatic Renewal- North America (G-CCRA-NA).

2010-2015: Representative of University of Chicago Medical Center at the Kenwood-Hyde Park Interfaith Council, Chicago, Illinois, USA.

August-November 2005: Staff Chaplain, Mercy Hospital, Chicago, Illinois, USA.

2003-2005: Registry Chaplain, University of Chicago Hospitals, Chicago, Illinois, USA.

1995-2001: Headmaster, Maranatha International School, Daban Panin-Kumasi, Ashanti Region, Ghana.

1991-1993: Headmaster, St. Louis Junior Secondary School, Mbrom-Kumasi, Ashanti Region, Ghana.

1990-1991: Diocesan Development Officer, Sunyani Catholic Diocese, Sunyani, Brong Ahafo Region, Ghana.

1974-1984: Headteacher, Catholic Primary School, Hwidiem, Brong Ahafo Region, Ghana.

1974, September-October: Teacher, Catholic Primary School, Ahafo Kenyasi II, Brong Ahafo Region, Ghana.

1974-2016: Counselor and Spiritual Director & Chaplain, Evangelist/Preacher/Conference Speaker, Volunteer Church Worker in Parishes, Churches, and Ministries.

Author's Profile

Recommended Books for Further Professional And Spiritual Development

1. *Integral Pastoral Care in Ghana: Proposals for Healing in the Asante Context by Gabriel Amoateng-Boahen.*
2. *The "Culture of Silence" Contributes to Perpetuating Domestic Violence: A Case Study of Family Life in the Brong Ahafo Region of Ghana by Gabriel Amoateng-Boahen.*
3. *Spiritual Mentorship for Pastors and Church Leaders Today by Gabriel Amoateng-Boahen.*
4. *My Ministry is Where My Mystery Was by Gabriel Amoateng- Boahen.*
5. *Pastoral Care and Holistic Ministry by Gabriel Amoateng-Boahen.*
6. *The Controlling Power Of The Mind: Renewing Your Mind Unto Victory by Gabriel Amoateng-Boahen.*
7. *African Punctuality: Time Is Divine And Of The Greatest Essence by Gabriel Amoateng-Boahen.*
8. *Testimonies Today Tributes Tomorrow by Gabriel Amoateng-Boahen.*
9. *The Theology Of my Life: From Kintampo To Chicago by Gabriel Amoateng-Boahen.*
10. *The Theology of Telephone Technology Today by Gabriel Amoateng-Boahen.*
11. *Spiritual Labour Room: Travailing Prayer by Veronica Amoateng Antwi.*
12. *Guarding and Protecting Your Prophetic Word by Daniel Amoateng.*
13. *Dreams and Their Interpretations by Daniel & Brian Amoateng.*
14. *From Impossibilities to Possibilities by Daniel Amoateng.*
15. *500 Wise Words and Life Lessons by Daniel Amoateng.*
16. *Daily Prophetic Declarations by Daniel Amoateng.*
17. *Exposing Dream Killers by Daniel Amoateng.*
18. *Why Was I Born? by Daniel Amoateng.*
19. *Favour by Brian Amoateng.*
20. *100 Wisdom Tablets by Brian Amoateng.*
21. *Hindrances to Prayer by Brian Amoateng.*
22. *5 Mistakes to Avoid in Life by Brian Amoateng.*
23. *You Can Recover From a Fall by Brian Amoateng.*
24. *Walking in the Favour of God by Brian Amoateng.*

25. *Dreams and Their Interpretations by Brian Amoateng.*
26. *Favor, Your key to Lasting Success by Brian Amoateng.*
27. *Answers God Gives When We Pray by Brian Amoateng.*
28. *Keys to Effective Travelling Ministry by Brian Amoateng.*
29. *The Wonders of Speaking in Tongues by Mark Amoateng.*
30. *How to Receive from God by Mark Amoateng.*
31. *The Law of Seed by Sampson Amoateng.*
32. *Possessing the Kingdom by Jesse Sackey.*
33. *Understanding the Divine Timing of God by Victor Owusu-Teng.*
34. *Understanding Your Divine Calling & Purpose by Victor Owusu-Teng.*
35. *Mission–Minded Skits by Cynthia Miller.*
36. *Mission-Minded Skits by Cynthia Miller.*
37. *Practical Psychology for Pastors by William R. Miller.*
38. *Called to Care: A Christian Theology of Nursing by Arlene B. Miller.*
39. *Restoring Fallen Pastors by Eric Reed.*
40. *Beyond Suffering by Joni Eareckson Tada.*
41. *Pastoral: An Essential Guide by John Patton.*
42. *Prayer: The 30 Most Powerful by John Bernthal.*
43. *The Strategically Small Church by Brandon O'Brien.*
44. *Leadership: Be Humble, Stay Hungry by Brad Lomenick.*
45. *Personal Identity in Theological Perspective by Richard Lints.*
46. *Dangerous Calling: Confronting the Unique by Paul David Tripp.*
47. *In the Name of Jesus Reflections by Henri J. M. Nouwen.*
48. *The Emotionally Healthy Leader: How to Leader by Peter Scazzero.*
49. *Being a Pastor: Understanding Our calling and Work by Derek J. Prime.*
50. *Ministerial Ethics: Moral Formation for Church Leaders by Joe E. Trull.*
51. *Pastoral Care in Context: An Introduction to Pastoral Care by John Patton.*
52. *Fivefold Ministry Made practical: How to Release Apostles, Prophets, Evangelists, Pastors, and Teachers to Equip Today's Church by Ron Myer.*
53. *The Right One: How to Successfully Date and Marry the Right Person by Jimmy Evans and Frank Martin.*
54. *Is God Calling Me?: Answering the Question Every Leader Believer Asks by Jeff Lorg.*

55. *Brothers, We Are Not Professionals: A Plea to Pastors for Radical Ministry* by John Piper.
56. *Be Thou Prepared: Equipping the Church for Persecution and Times of Trouble* by Carl Gallups.
57. *Practical Wisdom for Pastors: Words of Encouragement and Counsel for a Lifetime* by Curtis C. Thomas.
58. *Mentoring Leaders: Wisdom for Developing Character, Calling, and Competency* by Carson Pue.
59. *Preaching: Communicating Faith in an Era of Skepticism* by Timothy Keller.
60. *The Wounded Healer: Ministry in Contemporary Society* by Henri J.M. Nouwen.
61. *Pastoral Bearings: Lived Religion and Pastoral Theology* by Leonard Hammel.
62. *Professional Spiritual and Pastoral Care: A Practical Clergy and Chaplains' Handbook.*

Donations

Donations Accepted at http://donations.ghanarodi.org

Website: www.ghanarodi.org

E-Mail: gabriel@ghanarodi.org

       gabriel.ab925@yahoo.com

       gabrielabm1913@gmail.com

Chicago: Tel: 773-968-1983, 773-363-7889

Ghana: Tel: 020-812-1463, 020-783-0406, 020-783-0000

To Order Copies Of My Books In Chicago
Kilimanjaro International, Hyde Park

1305 East 53rd Street

Chicago, IL 60615

Tel: 773-324- 4860

Email: katumba2@alive.com

Xlibris Publishers

1-888-795-4274

To Order Copies Of My Books Online
Orders@Xlibris.com

www.Xlibris.com

www.amazon.com

www.barnesandboble.com

Available Formats: EBook, Audio Book, Paper and Hard Cover.

Rehoboth House Online Distributors

www.amazon.com

https://www.eden.co.uk

http://www.powells.com

http://www.audible.com

www.barnesandboble.com

http://www.christianbook.com

http://www.booksamillion.com/books

http://www.deepershopping.com/books.html

Available Formats: EBook, Audio Book, Paper and Hard Cover.

Mrs. *Agatha Amoateng-Boahen*

Author's Profile

Dr. Gabriel Amoateng-Boahen

www.ingramcontent.com/pod-product-compliance
Lightning Source LLC
Chambersburg PA
CBHW060459080526
44584CB00015B/1481